Nobody knows the truth but her

The Silent Witness

CASEY WATSON

This book is a work of non-fiction based on the author's experiences.
In order to protect privacy, names, identifying characteristics,
dialogue and details have been changed or reconstructed.

HarperElement
An imprint of HarperCollins*Publishers*
1 London Bridge Street
London SE1 9GF

www.harpercollins.co.uk

First published by HarperElement 2017

3 5 7 9 10 8 6 4

A catalogue record of this book is
available from the British Library

PB ISBN 978-0-00-814264-3
EB ISBN 978-0-00-814265-0

Printed and bound in Great Britain by
Clays Ltd, St Ives plc

MIX
Paper from
responsible sources
FSC® C007454

FSC™ is a non-profit international organisation established to promote
the responsible management of the world's forests. Products carrying the
FSC label are independently certified to assure consumers that they come
from forests that are managed to meet the social, economic and
ecological needs of present or future generations,
and other controlled sources.

Find out more about HarperCollins and the environment at
www.harpercollins.co.uk/green

The Silent Witness

To all the selfless people out there, in all walks of life. When you wonder whether or not your contribution makes a difference, please know that it does. Every act of kindness or compassion touches someone in some way, and down the line it will be remembered and reflected upon. As always, I'd like to give a special mention to those that work with children and spend every day trying to make a difference – I'm with you every step of the way.

Acknowledgements

Forever grateful to the team at HarperCollins for continuing to have faith in me and for helping me to get my stories out there. During hard times and good I have felt supported and inspired to carry on. Thanks also to my wonderful agent, Andrew Lownie, who never falters in his faith in me. I owe him everything! Finally, special thanks to my inspiration, mentor and good friend, Lynne, who keeps me plodding on regardless, and helps me to always see the sunny side.

Chapter 1

Christmas Eve. Early evening. Tools downed. To-do lists ticked. And to say I was excited is a bit of an understatement. I had begged. I had pleaded. I had wheedled and I had whined. And in the end, because there was clearly going to be no stopping me, Mike had caved in and let me open my main present early.

Just ten minutes ago, in fact, accompanied by heartfelt groans from Tyler, whose early mortification had just been endorsed by my first effort at channelling Beyoncé.

Yes, it had happened. I'd got my wish. My very own karaoke machine.

'*What*?' I asked Tyler, who was staring at me open-mouthed, and not, from the look of it, in a complimentary way. But why the face? He'd been our foster son for a good few years now. Our *son* now. He already *knew* about my singing abilities.

About which term we had to agree to disagree. I believed I had some, hence my list for Father Christmas, whereas Tyler believed that I must be tone deaf. 'Mum!' he cried, sounding mortified. 'Have you *listened* to yourself? *Ever?* Seriously,' he added, glancing at Mike, whereupon they shook heads in unison, 'you *need* to.'

'Well, exactly,' I said, beaming, despite the assault on my singing confidence. 'That's precisely why I needed to open it tonight. Plenty of time to get some practice in before tomorrow's singalong.'

Tyler picked up a cushion and covered his face with it, groaning, as any self-respecting fifteen-year-old boy would in such a circumstance. Though he still managed to guffaw from behind it when Mike added thoughtfully that it was less Beyoncé than a pastiche of early Shirley Bassey with a touch – a big touch – of Lee Marvin. I didn't care. I had a karaoke machine and I wasn't afraid to use it. I riffled through the choices and prepared to delight them with some Streisand. And got a belt with Tyler's cushion by way of gratitude.

I didn't care. I didn't mind. Exchanges like these were some of the greatest joys of family life. Not just the big things – the big moments, the overt displays of affection – but also the little things. The everyday and the largely unremarkable. Such as the gentle banter that thrives in an atmosphere of love and harmony. The gentle ribbing. The wordplay. The giggles and all the nonsense. It was Christmas Eve and all was well in my world.

Not that I was consciously thinking about that. I was too busy responding via the medium of song. But was saved, then, from further familial abuse by the sound of my mobile phone ringing. 'That'll be Riley,' I said, putting my microphone down and heading towards the dining room to take the call. She'd doubtless be calling with some last-minute directive or other, having summoned us to her house at silly o'clock the following morning.

Riley and her partner David had blessed us with three grandchildren by now – Levi and Jackson, who were ten and eight respectively, and the little mischief-making machine that was their youngest, Marley Mae, who was three going on the usual thirteen.

In previous years, we'd done things differently on Christmas morning. Now they were a bit older, they would generally open their presents at home (no sense getting the grandparents up at 4 a.m. when you have two parents already there for the purpose) and then coming over to ours mid-morning for another gift-opening session with Tyler and our other grandchild, Kieron and Lauren's darling little Dee Dee.

This year, however, it was all change. David's parents, who lived some way away now, were staying over with them, and it had been decided (unilaterally, because that's my Riley, bless her) that we should join them at hers for a big Christmas breakfast, so we could chat about Riley and David's upcoming wedding before they left for home.

The wedding was to be in February – scheduled for Valentine's Day. I couldn't have been more excited about that either. Oh, yes, all was very well with my world.

But it wasn't Riley. It was a male voice. One I recognised immediately as that of my fostering link worker, John Fulshaw, even though a glance at the clock made his call something of a shock. He'd already delivered my Christmas poinsettia, after all, and, as far as I knew, all was quiet on the fostering front.

It clearly wasn't. 'I'm so sorry, Casey,' he said. He sounded weary. 'I know this is probably the very worst time I could ring you, but we really are stuck. I mean *really* stuck. We desperately need someone to take a child this evening. As soon as possible in fact.'

Mike, from the sofa, mouthed the words 'What's wrong?' I mouthed back 'Emergency'. Enough said. Tyler, all ears now, turned the television down.

'Well, yes,' I said, eyeing my abandoned microphone sadly. 'But that's okay. Go on, tell me then. What's up?'

It was a short call, because this was clearly no time for rambling on. Suffice to say, I would now be working this Christmas. Mike and I both would. And all of us, because that's the nature of the job, would in all likelihood have our Christmas plans changed. We would be looking after a twelve-year-old girl, who was apparently called Bella, and who'd already been in the care system for a week. The details were sketchy (the usual 'I'll fill you in once we're sorted') but the gravity of the situation was not. Bella was in care because her stepfather was in a coma on a ventilator in an intensive therapy unit, having been put there with a life-threatening head injury, which had apparently been inflicted by Bella's mother. Attempted murder, by all accounts, which Bella had apparently witnessed, and while her stepdad fought for his life her mother was in prison.

People often ask me what kind of circumstances lead to a child being placed in care, and much of the time my responses are broadly similar. Abuse features regularly, as – equally depressingly – does neglect. The children of addicts, the children of virtual children themselves, the children who've been abandoned, those whose families have imploded or disappeared – the list of childhood miseries sometimes seems endless. But this was a new one. The grimmest kind of new one, to me anyway. Because the child who was coming to us had witnessed her mother attempting to kill her stepfather. Where did you start to imagine the myriad ways she must be in agony?

And on Christmas Eve, too. Yes, just another day, but a day that was marked in most calendars every year, which for a child was a treasure trove of happy memories. It didn't matter in the scheme of things what the date was. Of course it didn't. But if her stepdad died tonight, and her mother was convicted of murder, Christmas would be bound up with horrible memories for ever more.

'Yes, of course,' I told John, as soon as he'd finished filling me in. 'If there's no one else willing or able, of course we'll take her.'

'You don't know *how* relieved I am to hear that,' he told me. I knew he meant it, too. 'I'll pop an email to you now,' he added. 'You know, just outlining what I've told you, and with whatever else I can find out. Ten minutes, I promise. Pronto.'

'No worries,' I said. 'We can chat when you get here.'

'I can't,' he said. 'That's the thing. I *have* to get home. I am *so* sorry, Casey, but between you and me I shouldn't be here at all. I'm only in now because I forgot to switch my bloody mobile off. And here I am, passing the buck to you.'

I sympathised. I knew how guilty he must feel. I also knew just how many hours he clocked up in a week, many of them extremely unsociable ones, too – because fostering emergencies didn't keep office hours and, because that's the way life worked, often happened in the small hours, in the darkness before dawn, when the pubs turned out, the drug deals were completed, when reason went and tempers began fraying. And the wives and children of people with jobs like John's mattered too. I knew full well how little they got to see of him.

'No need to apologise,' I reassured him. 'Go on, get yourself home, okay?'

'That's the plan,' he said. 'Fingers crossed. Before I'm lynched! Bella's social worker, who's on her way to get her now, will bring her over to you, if that's okay. Hour or so. Two at the most. I'll double check and confirm in the email. Really, Casey, thanks so much for this. Terrible timing. And thanks to Mike, too.'

'No, it's *fine*,' I reassured him, before putting the phone down.

'No it's not,' Mike said immediately, as I walked back into the living room. My turn to face the music now, I realised. I knew I shouldn't have said yes. Not without checking with Mike first. But I knew that if I did check he'd say yes too. So not doing so was a time-saving exercise, that was all. 'It's Christmas *Eve*, love,' he said, not yet knowing the circumstances. 'Wasn't there anyone else John could ask?'

'If there had been, he wouldn't have called us, would he?' I told him reasonably. Though Mike did have a point. She wouldn't be the first child to have been deposited with us close to Christmas. But *this* close? John had said she was already in the system, hadn't he? So what had happened? Had another foster family decided they couldn't keep her?

I decided not to tell Mike about that part. Just the facts. An episode of violence (I was necessarily editing as I went, for Tyler's benefit). Dad in hospital. Mother in jail. And her a witness to it all, to her family falling apart. To her father's last hours of life, even, potentially. The poor child, we agreed, must be in bits.

And it wasn't like we had anyone in at the moment, was it? Bar Tyler, who no longer counted, of course, on account of being one of the family now. It had been a while, in fact, since we'd had anything approaching a long-term placement. Since Adrianna, a lovely Polish teenager, had left us at the end of spring, we'd only had children come to us on a short-term basis, keeping us free for the sort of child who needed specialist care long term.

This wasn't being billed as that, exactly, but, given the gravity of the circumstances, it might well turn out to be, mightn't it? Specially given John's email, which pinged into my inbox five minutes later, and, though brief, did make mention of Bella's demeanour, her probable post-traumatic stress disorder and her refusal to say a single word about what she'd seen. Emotionally shut down. Eating poorly. Unreachable. Deeply distressed.

'Well, that's Riley's breakfast off the agenda,' Mike said when I'd finished, ever the practical one. 'We'd better give her a ring and let her know.'

'She might like it,' Tyler suggested. 'Take her mind off stuff and that.'

'She might,' Mike conceded. 'Though by the sound of things Christmas will be the last thing on her mind. After all, she's –'

'Oh, *lord*,' I said, a thought having just occurred to me. 'Presents. She'll need some presents. Mike, we have to get her some presents.' I checked the time again. 'The supermarket. The supermarkets will still be open, won't they? For another hour, at least, anyway. Mike,' I went on, seeing his pained expression, 'I can't have a child here with nothing to open on Christmas morning. I just can't. Look, please, love. There's still time. You go off and get some bits for her while I go and sort the room out –'

'*Me*? Case, how am I supposed to know what to get a twelve-year-old girl?'

'Use your imagination,' I said, while grabbing his trainers so he could put them back on. 'Use Tyler's. Ty, you'll go with Dad, won't you? And I'll make a list. Let me see … pyjamas. She'll need some anyway, probably, as I don't have anything the right size. A dressing gown. A fluffy one. Some CDs. Some smellies … Get some paper, Ty. Write it down. Go on, quickly, the pair of you. You know what's current, Tyler … actually, on second thoughts, you can stay here with me. Help me clear all the rubbish in the bedroom …'

'And clean it to within an inch of its life,' he said, grinning. 'I know the drill, sir.' He clicked his heels.

'Cheeky tyke,' I said, aiming a gentle swipe at him. He was such a good boy. Such a lovely nature about him. Whatever else was true, Tyler's presence was a bonus for any child who came to us.

I bundled Mike out into the fairy-light spangled night, which was cloudless and chilly, then ran around, first pulling out my wrapping box so I could wrap up all the spoils,

8

then grabbing cleaning spray and dusters, and heading off up the stairs with Tyler to make the required assault on our unexpected charge's place of safety.

'Business as usual, then,' Tyler said, grinning as he unwound the cord on the vacuum cleaner.

I couldn't imagine anything about Bella's circumstance that merited anything other than heartbreak, but this was not the time for that. Place of safety, place of calm. I smiled back at Tyler. 'Yes, business as usual, love,' I agreed.

Chapter 2

I stared at my laptop screen, engrossed. While Mike was still out, and Tyler was ensconced in front of the telly, a second, more informative email had come through from John. And with coffee made, and the practical side of things finished, I had sat down to read it, first taking in the fact that it was so much longer than the first, and then, line by line, as it began to sink in, the truly desperate nature of this child's situation.

There was also a good reason for Bella's emergency relocation, it turned out. After having been taken from the family home, and interviewed (fruitlessly), she'd initially been billeted with another foster family. They were a middle-aged couple who often took emergency placements, and the intention had been for her to stay with them at least till New Year, when the various agencies and departments who made decisions in such weighty matters were back open for business. At that point, the holidays over, the intention was to move her to a longer-term foster home while the police built their case against her mother. But nature had no concern for the smooth running of social services, and it so happened that the couple had a very pregnant daughter who lived some 150 miles away.

That shouldn't have been a problem in itself. The baby wasn't apparently due till late January, so there was no reason for the couple not to have Bella short term. However, a few hours back, the couple's daughter had gone into early labour, and with complications that meant the couple had no choice (as if they'd want one) but to jump in the car and make the journey to be with her. Which left Bella out on a limb, since there was no guarantee they'd be back any time soon, which was where social services, and then John, and then Mike and I came in.

I sent up a silent prayer for happy news – perhaps a Christmas Day delivery? And for a baby who was delivered safe and well.

Then my thoughts naturally moved to the girl we were receiving. John had managed to speak at greater length with Bella's social worker's line manager, and was able to give me a fuller account of the events that had led to Bella being in care.

It seemed her mother, Laura Daniels, and her stepfather, Adam Cummings, had always had a volatile relationship. Together since Bella was three or four (with the stepdad acting very much as Bella's father, apparently), they were already known to social services and had been for some years, following numerous complaints to police and social services, mostly with regard to their frequent noisy rows. Screaming episodes, fighting in the garden, bouts of drunken brawling; incidents like these had seen them visited by those in officialdom on numerous occasions. It had apparently been a regular occurrence.

Yet on every occasion, it seemed, there was little in the way of follow-up. Which was not to say anything *should* have been done (all too easy to think you know better with the benefit of hindsight) but there was obviously a pattern: the mother always trying to calm the situation down and the stepfather, once questioned, always taking full responsibility, saying he had a drink problem which he was anxious to address.

I had heard it all before. Who hadn't? The cycle of drinking, drying out and then, down the line, the almost inevitable relapse was one that, sadly, was familiar to many. Yet it seemed there was a genuine desire to stop drinking in Adam Cummings, which was presumably why his luckless partner kept sticking by him. Which she clearly had, and, that being so, social services had taken a back seat, and their input had become minimal; at the time of this potentially lethal bout of violence they were down to twice-yearly visits. And all had been well. Well, up until a week ago, that was.

I wondered what had changed. What had finally broken her.

The one positive (in a situation where it looked like there was a distinct lack of positives) was that, by all accounts, Adam Cummings had never once laid a hand on Bella. That was also borne out by the observations of both the neighbours and successive social workers; Bella had always been found to be well looked after, well spoken, well turned out and clearly loved by both parents. Mum had always been apparently reasonably hands-on at Bella's primary school, too. And from discussions with the wider family, which apparently included the maternal grandparents (no mention of any family on his side), it was evident that Adam only ever lashed out when under the influence, and as Bella had apparently confirmed herself, never towards her. There was also a footnote – at the time of writing, which had been in early autumn, Adam had apparently been going to AA meetings regularly.

Ah, but Christmas. Bringer of joy, but also bringer-on of family tensions. And now a man lay in ITU and a woman in a prison cell. And in the midst of it all was their child, now all alone.

I heard the door open and close then. Time to ponder some more later. In the meantime there were presents to wrap. Hopefully.

My husband had done pretty well. 'Ah, brilliant,' I said repeatedly, as he produced gifts one by one from the supermarket carrier bag, like a conjuror pulling a rabbit from a hat. 'I'm sure she'll love that. And that. Oh, and that one, for definite.'

'And definitely these,' Tyler contributed, having wrenched himself from the TV to lend his considered opinion of Mike's choice of music CDs.

CDs were still something of a staple in our fostering lives, as we still had two elderly CD players; one in what was now Tyler's room – he didn't use it but wouldn't part with it – and the other in the spare, fostering, bedroom. Yes, very old-school, and often the subject of amusement among the young ('CD player? Isn't that, like, an *antique*?'

or, in one memorable case, 'What *is* that?') but while music was universal, the modern kit on which to play it was often not – not for some of the kids who had passed through our doors down the years; some barely had shoes, let alone iPods and iPhones. We also – old school again – still had two DVD players.

'Not sure about *that*, though,' Tyler sniffed, catching the fluffy pink rabbit Mike now did, in fact, produce from the bag and throw at him.

'It's to put on her bed, *stoopid*,' he said. 'You've got to learn how girls operate, mate. Stuff on beds. That's their thing. Totally pointless, but completely indispensable. Am I not right, oh noble Cushion Queen? Isn't that exactly what girls do?'

I laughed. 'It's *exactly* what girls do,' I said.

As well as the CDs and the fluffy bunny, and some appropriately pink festive toiletries, there was also a dressing gown – also pink and fluffy – a pair of butterfly-strewn pyjamas, a set of various hair bobbles and clips, and what I'd thought was the latest Harry Potter book – *The Order of the Phoenix* – which, according to a laughing Tyler, wasn't very 'latest' these days, but was a bargain, apparently, and would definitely double up as a doorstop if she'd already read it.

I reached for the wrapping paper, and handed scissors and ribbon to Tyler. 'I'll wrap, you garnish,' I said, which always made him giggle. 'Remember the way I showed you how to curl the ribbon?'

'*Course*,' he said. (In fact he was something of a natural.) 'But I swear to God, don't ever tell any of my mates I do stuff like this. Especially Denver. I'd *never* live it down.'

Denver was Tyler's best friend – had been for a few years now. He was a lovely boy and, from the start, he had been so good for Ty, particularly during the early days when he so missed his younger brother, who was still with his father and (to my mind) wicked stepmother. Ty and Denver had a bond now that I'd stake my life would prove unbreakable. And despite their endless quest to create some kind of hard-man image in public, they were both very similar in nature: kind-hearted and loving kids.

'I swear on everything swearable on that your secret is safe with me,' I told him. 'Just like I've never told him you still have your bedtime milk in a plastic Spiderman cup.'

'*Mother!*' Tyler yelled, making me smile even more. The longer he was with us, the more he became just like us. A natural phenomenon, of course, but still thrilling even so. Not least because he sounded so like our Kieron at that age. Our Kieron who was now a fully grown, fully wise twenty-seven-year-old with a toddler. One of the joys of fostering, without a doubt, was the privilege (which was what it felt like to me) to live so many special parenting moments again.

But a great deal of what we did was about the bad times rather than the good times, and, the presents wrapped and the clock ticking – it was by now after 10 p.m. – it was at the front of my mind that our young visitor still hadn't arrived yet.

By ten o'clock I was getting more than a bit antsy. Bella *still* hadn't arrived and though I knew everything would change as a consequence of her coming to us, we still had to eat, and we still had to celebrate Christmas, albeit in perhaps a less OTT, more thoughtful fashion. Which meant I still had lots of preparation to do for the next day's big celebratory dinner. I had the turkey to sort out, the vegetables to peel and the stuffing to make. The more I thought about it, the more panicked I was getting, not least because we still hadn't made a firm plan for the morning either. Yes, I'd texted Riley, but we'd settled on a 'we'll see' scenario, which left an item not ticked off my mental to-do list – always a recipe for ants in the pants.

But such is human nature. Despite the momentous events that had happened in the life of the girl who was on her way to us, which, by any yardstick, made worries about having the stuffing ready ridiculous, it was human nature for me to focus on the practical. What was the saying? Not 'don't sweat the small stuff' – I couldn't help doing that. No, the one about not worrying about the things you couldn't control, and sticking to the ones that you could.

So it was that I had both hands in a bowl of sausage meat and breadcrumbs when my mobile went again. It was getting on for eleven – and it was John, despite his assurance that he'd clocked off hours ago.

Mike was in the living room watching TV and Tyler was now in bed, so I picked it up gingerly with my greasy hands.

'John, honestly,' I berated him. 'You are supposed to be off duty.'

'I know, I know,' he said. 'And the wife's probably busy plotting ways to kill me. But I had to ring; didn't think you'd be logging on to read your email.'

'No, you're right,' I said. 'I actually had my hands in the stuffing. Hang on for ten seconds, can you, while I scrape them clean?'

That job done, we returned to the matter in hand. And the news that Bella had been delayed by the need for a whopping diversion, to collect the presents that had apparently already been bought and wrapped for her and were stashed at the family home in her parents' wardrobe.

'Bit eleventh hour,' I remarked. 'How come that hadn't happened in the first place?'

'Message only just got through from Laura Daniels's lawyer,' John explained. 'So the whole thing has turned into something of an epic journey. Latest ETA is still an hour or so from now. So Christmas Day, in fact. What a game this is, eh? Had to be done, though.'

'Yes, had to be done,' I agreed. And despite the late arrival, I was glad for her. She would at least have that connection to her parents to hang on to; however things panned out – and, knowing the odds when it came to head injuries bad enough to warrant a bed in ITU, it was probably all going to pan out pretty wretchedly – that connection to those closest to her was still important. And who knew how important it would be in the coming days and weeks? There was no guarantee her stepfather would even live, after all.

'And something else,' John said, pulling me back from my reverie. 'The main reason I called, actually. Another snippet of information. I've been able to chat to Sophie's line manager, Kathy –'

'Sophie?' I'd not come across a Sophie in the line of duty before.

'Sophie is Bella's social worker. Sorry – didn't I say? You'll like her. Anyway, it seems the first port of call when this whole thing blew up was the grandparents – Laura Daniels's parents, that is – who were happy to take Bella in.'

'But obviously didn't.'

'Exactly. Because Bella wouldn't hear of it. I mean, *seriously* wouldn't hear of it, by all accounts. To the point of becoming hysterical. Said she'd rather go to strangers than have to live with her granddad.'

My antennae started twitching immediately. 'Really?'

'Yes, too frightened of him. She was apparently quite open about it, too. No allegations of anything inappropriate – nothing like that's been suggested, and he's not known to social services or anything. But all's clearly not well where the family is concerned. She's close enough to the grandmother to spend time with her reasonably regularly, but neither Bella *nor* her mother see anything of the grandfather. Never go to the house. There's obviously some kind of rift there. Course, it might not have any bearing on anything, but I thought it worth you knowing. It's another piece of the jigsaw at least, isn't it?'

I agreed that it was. And he was right. It was definitely worth us knowing. How it affected anything I didn't know, but it all added to the picture. And one thing I'd learned a very long time ago was that there was rarely smoke without at least a small hint of a fire. Time would tell. I signed off with a 'Don't you dare ring me again till at *least* the 27th,' then put my head round the kitchen door and summoned my husband. I needed a kitchen hand, a confidant and coffee.

Chapter 3

It was almost midnight when we heard the car pull up and both Mike and I hurried to peek out of the window.

Mike whistled, long and low. 'Wow,' he said. 'Social workers must be on some good pay these days. I'd give anything for a car like that.'

He then fell silent – out of respect – as the black BMW convertible finished its manoeuvre into the just-big-enough space under the street lamp outside our frost-bitten front garden.

I tutted and pulled a face at him, as I often had to do, if only in support of our own elderly car, which was sitting hunched on the driveway, and no doubt feeling very inadequate in the face of so much beauty. 'Nothing wrong with our old reliable,' I reminded him. 'It gets us from A to B, and it suits me just fine, thank you very much.'

'I know,' he said. 'But a man can dream, can't he?'

We had to dart backwards then, sharpish, as the driver door opened and a woman stepped out. 'Honestly, Mike,' I hissed. 'Look at us! We're like a pair of nosey old neighbours. Come on.' I yanked on his arm, and we hurried out into the hall, putting our best welcoming smiles on to greet our visitors.

The social worker was young, and very pretty. Even more so in the glow of my twinkling archway of outside fairy lights, which I'd agonised about leaving on or switching off out of respect for the gravity of our house guest's situation. It wasn't like me to dither, but I couldn't stop thinking that the poor girl's stepfather might die at any moment. (Lights *on*, Mike had decreed. Let's keep everything normal.)

'Hi,' I said, offering my hand to the social worker, who was carrying a supermarket 'bag for life' which presumably held Bella's presents. I then moved my gaze to the girl at her side, who was wearing a heavy winter coat, with the hood up. She looked slight for her age, with what looked like long, dark blonde hair – difficult to say how long, given the hood. She too had a bag – a black backpack, which she held at her side. 'And you must be Bella,' I said brightly. 'I'm Casey, and this is Mike. Come on in. You must be freezing, not to mention exhausted.'

I led them straight into the living room, a little concerned by the fact that Bella hadn't even looked up at me when I'd spoken to her, let alone said hello or anything else. She hung on to her backpack, and made no move to take her coat off, and not even a glance towards the enormous, all-singing, all-dazzling tree that currently dominated the room. She was simply afraid, I supposed, on top of everything else. Just as she was settled in one place, here she was being moved again. Shut down. That was what

John's email had said, hadn't it? Shut down and shut in. I didn't press it.

Instead I pointed out the sofa to the social worker, who'd introduced herself as Sophie Taylor, and shrugged off her overcoat to give to Mike, who had already taken the bag. She sat down and Bella immediately sat down next to her, keeping close, head still tucked down like a turtle's into the neck of her black winter coat. It had a thick collar of grey fur that provided the perfect hideaway for her little face.

'So,' I said to them both. 'A hot drink? You've had a long journey, haven't you?'

Bella's only response was to glance nervously at Sophie, who then nodded. 'Coffee would be manna from heaven, trust me. Thanks so much. And how about you, Bella? Cuppa tea?' She then turned back to me. 'Cup of tea, please. White, one sugar. Bella is a proper teapot.'

The girl didn't so much as move, let alone smile at this. 'Okay then,' I said, rubbing my hands together and looking at Mike. 'Shall you and I go and make some drinks, love, while Sophie and Bella warm up a little?'

Mike nodded eagerly, clearly feeling the tension too.

'God, she's young, isn't she?' he commented, as I rummaged in the cupboard for matching mugs.

'Who, Bella?'

'No, the social worker. *Sophie.*' He didn't need to add what I imagined he was thinking, which was how someone so young could be in possession of such a flashy car, while he was fifty-something and hadn't progressed beyond a family hatchback.

'She does look very young,' I agreed. 'Maybe she's very new to the job. Or maybe we're just losing track. Like policemen, aren't they? Just keep getting younger and younger.'

He smiled. 'Heaven forbid that it's us getting older, eh?'

But Sophie Taylor's youth – and likely lack of experience – didn't seem to affect her confidence. 'So,' she said, when we returned, bearing the designated refreshments, 'the famous Watsons! I'm so pleased to meet you. I've heard so much about you.' She looked towards Bella, and, smiling, continued, 'Casey and Mike have been fostering for ever such a long time, Bella. You're in very good hands, sweetheart. You'll love it here.'

It didn't quite seem the time to be singing our praises, nor being quite so gung-ho. Blasé, almost. After all, Bella was hardly going to 'love it'. She'd endure it as best she could, possibly even adjust to it eventually. But 'love it'? Under the circumstances, I didn't think so.

But perhaps I was being picky. The poor girl was doing her best to jolly things along. And judging by what I'd so far seen and heard had been doing so since the outset, and today, with all the upheaval, perhaps doing so for a good part of the day and evening. So she'd be tired too.

'You know what,' I said, once Mike had given Sophie her coffee. 'It's beyond silly o'clock now, and I, for one, am bushed. Which means you, Bella, must be absolutely exhausted, and not in the least interested in having to sit here and listen to the adults all blabbering on.' I stood up then, from where I'd perched on the edge of the adjacent armchair, took two steps and stuck a hand out in Bella's direction.

It was one of my tried and tested openers and was surprisingly effective. Not every time, but more than you'd expect given the situation – given that me and whichever child I was offering a hand to were complete strangers. But maybe not so surprising, given children's natural need for order and security. In some situations, and with some people – people in authority, like head teachers, nurses and foster carers – it was actually quite natural to take the adult's hand.

'Come on, sweetie,' I said, nudging the hand towards her, 'before we get roped into a very long night, let's me and you go up and see your room, shall we? And leave Mike and Sophie down here to chat.' I glanced meaningfully at Sophie then, because usual protocol was for the social worker to go up and look at the room initially, and her answering nod indicated she was happy with my suggestion. 'Then if you want to sneak into your bed,' I went on, still hoping Bella would put her hand in mine, 'that would be fine. Or just two minutes' peace and come back down. Entirely up to you.'

The wait for a reaction from her felt like for ever, but slowly, under the onslaught of words, presumably, Bella raised her little face from the nest of fur, revealing a pair of beautiful, wide blue eyes. She glanced at my hand nervously, but then – yes! – she took it, and allowed me to guide her, holding her tea in my free hand, past Sophie, past Mike, into the hall. 'Top of the stairs and turn left,' I said as she started up the stairs before me. 'I don't know what you like, Bella, but I'm forewarning you, it's very pink. You have any sunglasses?'

I was rewarded again then by a brief backwards glance, and though the fur was very thick and I didn't know if I'd raised a smile, it was at least an acknowledgement that I'd spoken. Progress of some sort at least.

Bella waited at the top of the stairs, head tucked back into her nest of fake fur, so I reached past her and opened the bedroom door for her. 'Go on in, love,' I said. 'All yours. I promise I won't pester you.' I then flicked on the light switch to illuminate where everything was and was pleased to watch Bella's chin inching out of the collar, as she turned her head and began taking it all in.

'So,' I said, since she clearly wasn't about to say anything. 'I'll leave you up here for a bit, shall I? The remote for the TV is on the dressing table, if you'd like to put it on. Though quietly' – I gestured back out towards the landing – 'because Tyler, our son, our *foster* son,' I qualified, thinking it might help reassure her, 'is in the room right over there. He's fifteen,' I added, realising she was finally looking at me. 'And a bit of a light sleeper. He can't wait to meet you.' I smiled and pointed to the little backpack she'd been clutching. 'Do you have your night-wear in that, or should I get something out for you? There are pyjamas in the chest of drawers over there.'

In answer, she shook her head and lifted the bag slightly. Which, again, was progress, even if not very much.

'Well, you get sorted then,' I said, stepping back out onto the landing. 'Bathroom's just over there, see? And it really is up to you. If you want to go to bed, then that's fine, but if you want to come back down again that's fine too. No sweat either way, sweetie. You do what you like tonight, all right?' I nodded towards the bedside table. 'And get that tea down you before it gets cold.'

A nod this time. I closed the door softly behind me.

I decided not to hang about, either. I suspected she'd need to hear I was actually back downstairs before she could properly relax, get undressed, use the bathroom or whatever, so I made a bit of a stomp about going back down so that she'd know she was safe to move around.

Back in the living room the mood, despite the light show, was darker.

'She's not spoken a word hardly,' Mike told me as soon as I entered. 'I was just asking Sophie about the post-traumatic stress thing, and apparently she's barely spoken since they took her.'

'I thought she might be, by now,' Sophie said, 'you know, since being with the other carers, but there's no change, not while we were there, not while we were waiting, not in the car. Not a single word, nothing. It's like she's mute.'

I had some experience with mutism from back during my days as a school behaviour manager. Not this kind of mutism, as in an extreme response to a trauma – the girl in my care had longstanding selective mutism, which only manifested itself while in school. But this kind – the 'response to severe stress' kind of mutism was, I'd read, a great deal more common. And it wasn't just that it had only been a matter of days, either – it was ongoing; she'd witnessed something no child should witness, and, to compound it, she was now being told what to do by complete strangers while her dad was in hospital and mum was in jail. It was a miracle she wasn't hysterical. She may yet be. These things could be episodic, ebbing and flowing, triggered by all sorts of things.

'It's understandable,' I said. 'It's a nightmare, all this, isn't it? And now, to compound it, she's been moved here, so it's like she's back to square one. And for who knows how long?'

'Mike was just asking me about that,' Sophie said. 'And the honest truth is that we have no idea.' She flicked her hair, which was long and dark, back across her shoulders. 'It's all so sad, isn't it? And no guessing what the outcome's going to be either. Still, soon as Christmas is over, we're arranging for Bella to see a counsellor. Which might help. We hope. There's no question of her being returned to her previous placement, by the way – John might have told you?'

'Oh no,' I said. 'What's happened? Have there been complications with the baby?'

Sophie shook her head. 'No, no – well, not as far as I know. No, they just don't have any idea when they'll return right now. And to be honest, even when they do they've already said they'd rather not have her back. They said they were struggling with her, to be honest – not sure they were the right couple for her. Just the three of them in the house, rattling around, Bella so silent. They feel she'd be better placed with a younger, busier family ...'

'We'll we're certainly busy,' Mike said.

'Excuse me? *And* young ...' I couldn't help adding.

'Exactly,' Sophie said. 'Which is why it's so great that you've said you'll have her. Big noisy family. Lots of distractions. Your other child – Tyler? It is Tyler, isn't it?' We both nodded. 'Let's hope they bond, eh? Oh, and that reminds me. I've already spoken to her about keeping off of social media. I don't know how much she uses it, because it's impossible to get anything out of her. But she's got an account – I checked – though I have no idea how much she uses it. Parents do too. So I've explained how it's important that she should avoid it – all the chitter-chatter and idle gossip and so on – and that if she wants to get in touch with friends, she needs to do it the old-fashioned way: putting pen to paper, through you. But you'll know all that anyway, of course. Sorry.' She gave an apologetic little grimace. I was really beginning to warm to her. 'Anyway, we really are incredibly grateful,' she finished. 'And I'm here, of course – well, I say "here", I need my bed now, as I'm sure you do. But you know, as a port of call – I'm on call right through Christmas. You know, if there are any problems that you need me for and so on … And I'm a constant,' she said. 'I've been assigned full time to Bella's case, so at least there's that.'

'That's good news,' I said, because it really was. I knew all too well that, in their early days in care, children often went through many different social workers. It was no one's fault. It was just that, often, there was simply no one free to take them on as a long-term commitment; caseloads were huge, always, and there was also the problem that a lot of the time no one knew how long a child was even going to be in the system. So it was often a case of filling in, helping out, the child being passed hither and thither, between social workers who already had way too much to do. And at Christmas, of course, all these problems were compounded. So, yes, it was indeed good that Bella already had that continuity in her social worker, even if Sophie might not be the most experienced one in the world.

But, arguably, she was at least the brightest.

'I've got to say, Casey,' she said, once she'd drained her mug and put her coat back on, 'your Christmas tree is *magical.*'

Which made me smile. At least till we waved Sophie off, and the reality set in. That I didn't have a magic wand to go with it.

Chapter 4

As far as I knew, Bella slept soundly through the night. Perhaps she was just as physically exhausted as she was emotionally, but on both occasions I checked on her – I couldn't sleep a wink, of course – I was actually surprised to find her dead to the world, star-fished on her back, snoring, one arm cradling a large and surprisingly ugly-looking soft toy – not one of ours – that looked a bit like a gremlin. Each to their own, I thought.

And both times I tiptoed in there it occurred to me that for the majority of kids, and the majority of the Western world, this was supposed to be a night of an excess of excitement, and of waking disgruntled parents long before dawn. Not so Bella. Not for many other hidden-from-view, desperate children. No happy family Christmas for them come the morning. I wondered where her mother was. What she was feeling. What a mess.

It was a far from normal Christmas morning in our house as well. Despite the lack of sleep, I'd left my alarm set for six thirty, knowing the hours ahead were going to be fraught, unknown territory. I was therefore anxious to steal a march on the day. And when it roused me – from one of those deep sleeps the sleepless always seem to fall into just before waking-up time – it was down to a cold, silent kitchen that I tiptoed, so I could get ahead with all the tasks I invariably had to do, before anyone else was awake.

Not that I expected Tyler to be that far behind me. He might be fifteen now and in theory too old to get over-excited about such childish pleasures, but, of course, many of his Christmas childhoods had been exercises in pure misery, as his father capitulated and let his stepmother bully him, while lavishing love and gifts on his younger half-brother. No, I didn't think he'd ever outgrow such a simple, precious pleasure. And, if I had any say in it, nor would he.

For now, though, I worked silently, with only the radio on low for company; doing all the jobs I'd generally be doing with the radio blaring (singing along, sometimes dancing, a small sherry at my elbow) knowing that across the hallway, in the living room, whatever collection of kids, foster kids and grandkids we had with us, there would be happy, wrapping-paper-strewn mayhem.

I could have almost become maudlin, thinking about the girl who had parachuted into our lives so unexpectedly, so it was a blessing that Mike and Tyler joined me a scant half hour later, both whispering about the new house guest and what might be going through her head, and wondering if she'd come down or if I should go and wake her.

Eventually – and after promising they'd help with any outstanding preparations – they bullied me into going up and bringing her downstairs. Which made sense. She was going to be a huge part of our lives over the coming days, and for who knew how much longer? So the sooner we settled her in with us, and she became familiar with all our little ways – and us hers – the better those few days would be for everyone.

Bella's bedroom door was shut when I got up to the landing, so I assumed she must have woken and perhaps used the bathroom, but when I knocked there wasn't any reply. I waited a moment or two, wondering if she might be in the middle of dressing, but when an ear to the door produced only silence, I knocked again, and this time I opened the door slightly as well.

'You awake, sweetie?' I asked her, popping my head around the jamb.

Evidently. Because she wasn't even in bed. In fact, it had already been neatly made, the weird soft toy I'd seen the night before sitting propped in front of the pillows.

'So who's this?' I went on brightly, the answer to my first question now being evident. 'Should we be formally introduced?'

Bella's only response was to give me a tight, if polite, smile. She was sitting at the dressing table, in the pink pyjamas and dressing gown she had presumably taken from her backpack, brushing her hair with a pink polka-dotted hairbrush (tick to me, regarding the pink, then). The hair itself was thick and blonde. And much longer than I'd realised. The sort of hair that in the future would be the envy of her friends. Friends. I made a mental note to ask Bella about them. Friends who could provide support and continuity. Some much-needed sense of normality. But perhaps not just yet. Though it occurred to me to find her some paper and pens, just in case. She might like to write to friends, at least. Not to mention her parents – and grandparents? I made a mental note to ask John about that.

'Anyway!' I said. 'Merry Christmas. Shall we go down so you can open your presents? Tyler's already down there,' I added, smiling relentlessly in the face of her scared, wary expression. 'Come on, poppet. Let's head downstairs, shall we? He's dying to meet you.'

Bella reddened slightly, whether in response to the mention of Tyler or just because she felt scrutinised I didn't know. She hadn't responded, much less moved – well, apart from the repetitive hair-brushing – so I went into the bedroom properly, then squatted down on my haunches beside the dressing table so I was on her level. Even below it, slightly – I'm not the tallest of people, and I was now almost looking up at her. And was also close enough to see the grey smudges of tiredness bruising the skin beneath her pale, frightened eyes.

'I know this is all very strange for you,' I said gently. 'And you must be feeling wretched, sweetheart. And scared, too. How could you be feeling anything else? But one thing I can tell you is that you have nothing to be frightened of here, okay? No one will make you do anything you don't want to, I promise. So, then. How about it? Shall we head down? Go downstairs and just see how it goes for a bit?' Silence. Just her face looking ahead, fixed firmly on her reflection, accompanied by the rhythmic strokes of the hairbrush. 'And, if it's all too much,' I went on, 'you can come back up for a bit, I promise.' I stood up again, and held my hand out, as I'd done the night before. 'What do you reckon, Bella? Is that a plan?'

Again that endless wait, but again, finally, it worked. She stood up, went across to the bed and grabbed the gremlin, then slipped, to my delight, her small, hot hand into mine. I squeezed it reassuringly, then led her straight down into the living room, and immediately across to the twinkling tree, where the presents we'd got her were all wrapped and had her name on – though, given how on edge (not to mention *the* edge) she probably was currently, I felt it probably prudent to let her make the running where it came to the gifts retrieved from her own home, and which were still in the corner, in the carrier bag they'd arrived in. I suspected that she might well prefer to open those ones in the privacy of her bedroom. Or, indeed, not open them at all.

'Go on,' I urged, as she once again gazed as if transfixed by the sight of the enormous twinkling tree, and the mound of gifts beneath it. 'Why don't you sit down on the rug and have a rootle round for the presents we've got for you while I go and get you some toast and hot chocolate. You like hot chocolate?' I added. And was rewarded by a minor miracle. She actually nodded. *Yes*.

I was just turning round to leave when Mike and Tyler appeared in the doorway. I saw Bella stiffen at the sight of them – or, perhaps, instinct told me, it was just Mike that made her stiffen, given his size, his maleness and the violence she'd so recently witnessed, so I signalled for him to do an about-turn and return to help me in the kitchen. 'Ah, here you are, Ty,' I said. 'This is Bella. Just about to start attacking her presents. You want to get stuck in with her as well? Go on, dig in. Make as much mess as you like.'

I had to smile then, as Tyler sank down onto his knees on the rug and grinned at her. 'Lols,' he said, smiling back at me, knowing full well I'd hear him. 'Hi, Bella. Now let's make Mum – make *Casey* – wish she'd never said that. First thing you need to know here. She absolutely *hates* mess.'

I grinned at him as I left them to it, but Tyler was wrong about that. At least on this particular occasion. On any other day of the year, yes, I'd be the first to admit that mess-management was a major factor in my life. Not an issue, exactly; we hosted all manner of mess-making activities, just like anyone else. It was just that I was a tiny bit obsessive about cleaning before anyone arrived and equally obsessive about tidying up after them once they'd gone, even if the 'going' bit took place at three in the morning. No biggie. That was just my little foible.

But Christmas was different. To my mind there were few things more sad and poignant than the sight of a Christmas living room devoid of kids unwrapping presents and throwing paper and packaging all around the place. Call me sentimental but it always seemed to me, at least for the precious couple of hours before they came up for air again, that while they were swimming joyfully in a sea of discarded wrappings I was bobbing on a little sea of happiness.

And Tyler made a good fist of making that happen. By the time Mike and I returned with drinks and toast to keep us going till the inevitably late Christmas dinner we were going to be having, given Riley's breakfast club, he'd wellied into most of the presents we'd allowed him to open without us with great excitement and gay abandon – we'd been able to hear his whoops of joy from the kitchen.

But that was all we heard. Though she was sitting passively and politely on the rug, having by now systematically piled her presents at her side, Bella seemed wedded to the idea of children being seen and not heard; at best she nodded in response to Tyler, offering no more communication than the odd ghost of a smile.

Tyler, for his part, carried gamely on. He seemed to have decided that he'd just fill the conversational gaps with yet more words and, in the absence of any other strategy, we took his lead, treating Bella almost – though without any lack of respect – like an amiable family dog, from whom we didn't actually expect any response.

We decided the best thing would be if I, and I alone, popped round to Riley's for an hour, on the basis that it was David's mum and I who'd be the most closely involved in the wedding preparations, discussion of which was the main reason for going round. It would also give me a chance to prepare the ground before they all descended on us – and Bella – at dinner-time, so that they understood that it would, of necessity, be a different kind of Christmas Day. It would also give me a chance to fill in Kieron and Lauren – also scheduled to come to us for Christmas dinner later.

I'd wavered a bit – another reason for my largely sleepless night – reasoning that one alternative would be to cancel the day altogether, for fear it might make Bella's emotional state even worse. It wasn't the first time we'd had a child in over Christmas and I doubted it would be the last, because Christmases are times of great stress and a key time for family breakdowns, but every situation was different, as was every child. Had things been less on a knife-edge – you didn't get more knife-edge than Dad in ITU and Mum in jail for trying to kill him, I reckoned – it would have been less difficult a decision, and had Bella been younger (say five or six) it would have been a completely different story; younger children, in my experience, were better able to distract themselves from the enormity of the life-change they were experiencing, as they were more able to 'park' it and make believe they were just off on some sort of holiday.

But would cancelling Christmas really help Bella anyway? Yes, she was clearly old enough to feel terrified about how her future was unravelling, but perhaps that meant she needed distraction even more.

There was also my own family to consider. And to cancel things would be to create a logistical nightmare, not least because I was the one with the turkey and all the trimmings, and to try and rejig and/or relocate the whole shebang would cause even more upheaval, not least because of the many comings and goings that it would require.

No, on balance, we agreed, we should probably press on with the day – envelope our frightened visitor in festive love and laughter, but with the safe haven of her bedroom, should she need it. She didn't strike me as a child who wanted to be the centre of attention, which the alternative scenario meant she would be.

And it was Bella herself who finally ticked the mental box. In the fact that, the presents opened (bar her own from her family, as yet) and the toast and hot chocolate dispatched, she seemed happy enough to curl up at one end of the sofa and settle down to watch a Harry Potter film with Tyler – and with her cherished soft toy – not a gremlin, but a 'Dobby the house-elf', according to Tyler – *and* the rabbit we'd got for her, which pleased me greatly. Indeed, I had much to thank J. K. Rowling for that morning, because it was a shared devotion to the young wizard that forged their first, tentative bond, and, in response to his 'Wicked! *The Deathly Hallows* is on. You want to watch it?' elicited her first proper words since she'd come to us, which were 'Yes, please.'

But which also caused me to wonder, as I drove the short distance to Riley's house, what kind of mutism we were actually dealing with here. My experience wasn't extensive – I'd only worked closely with one child who displayed similar systems, truth be told – but in doing so, I'd read up on different forms of mutism, and instinct told me this was more a conscious choice on Bella's part than anything else. This certainly didn't seem to fit the profile of other forms I'd come across, where the child struggled to overcome what was often a physiological as well as a psychological barrier, often unconscious. No, it was more that Bella had made a *very* conscious decision not to engage.

All very intriguing, and it didn't take a rocket scientist to work out that it was almost certainly because Bella had witnessed that attempted murder by her mother and was shutting down to avoid incriminating her further, during the endless questions she'd have doubtless already been asked in its aftermath.

Even so, there was a difference between refusing to discuss that, and making a blanket decision not to speak to anyone at all.

Riley, now a respite foster carer herself, agreed. 'Though let me be the first to suggest one minor change in tonight's entertainment,' she commanded. 'That the karaoke machine remains unplugged.' Which suggestion was naturally passed unanimously.

'Seriously,' she added, 'I think you're right to stick with the plan, Mum, and I'm not just saying that because I don't want to give up my Christmas dinner.' ('Oh, yes, you are,' came the rousing chorus from around the table.) 'I reckon she can distract herself better in a big crowd of kids than if she's got everyone's attention on her in a silent empty house. Didn't you just say that was why things weren't working out in the last foster place she was at? I know that's how I'd feel, anyway. Specially given that every adult she's had anything to do with up till now has probably been trying to get her to talk about what happened. I wonder what *did* happen ...' she mused. 'Do you reckon her mother *was* trying to kill him?'

It was obviously impossible to answer that question till one of two things happened – either Bella's father recovered sufficiently to recount the facts as he remembered (as best he could, given that one fact we did know was that he was extremely drunk when admitted to A&E), or Bella herself decided to. As things stood, her mum was pleading hitting him in self-defence, and until her partner's situation resolved itself – either he recovered or he died – there was nothing to be done. I wondered if Bella herself was almost in a state of mental breath-holding. I wondered how she felt about her dad's possible death. How she felt about her dad.

I didn't stay long at Riley's – really only long enough to talk wedding to-do lists with David's mum. And, once I was back home, knowing the entire family were going to be with us in a scant three or four hours – not to mention our first foster child, Justin, now a strapping adult, with an appetite to match – I took advantage of Bella's apparent desire to stay on the sofa in her pyjamas to properly attack all the food preparation. Every time I checked on her, she was either watching TV with Tyler, or had her nose in a Harry Potter book; it seemed he'd brought down the entire collection from his bedroom, and that though she'd told him she'd read them all – some of them twice (positively chatty now, at least with Ty!) – she'd be more than happy to read them all again.

But if that had been Bella's escape plan (and a book was always an excellent escape plan) the combined onslaught of attention from my quartet of noisy grandchildren proved too powerful a force to avoid. Very soon, though still largely silent and wary around the adults, she was immersed in their world of make-believe and dolls and Lego, and though she still didn't speak much she was at least fully engaged – well, again, as far as I could tell.

I sat her next to Levi for our Christmas dinner, since, my eldest grandchild being ten now, they were closest in age, but it was soon clear that the closest bond she was likely to forge was with Marley Mae. From the outset, Bella had been my granddaughter's main topic of interest, and was fast becoming her little shadow.

'I think it's because she can't ask her anything she doesn't want to answer,' I told Lauren, my Kieron's other half, while we stacked and put away the dishes the men had washed up. 'That's my take on it, anyway.' Lauren and Kieron's Dee Dee was also monopolising this young stranger, though she was currently spark out, having her nap on Kieron's chest. At only two, she still needed to take such power naps when in the company of her boisterous older cousins. 'Makes sense, doesn't it? I mean, I know the older children don't know what's happened, but they'll be curious, won't they? And, in Levi's case, particularly, doing the whole twenty questions thing. Give him a fair wind, and he'd have everything out of her, from what her favourite colour is to which character she'd be in Minecraft.'

Lauren nodded. 'I think you're right. Whereas Marley Mae is more like an adoring puppy. Correction – more accurately, adoring limpet mine.'

And it wasn't just that, truth be known. With her admirable sleuthing skills, Marley Mae had sniffed out the bag of unopened presents in the corner almost as soon as she'd finished opening hers. And, working on the basis that an unopened present on Christmas night was a crime against all humanity, had badgered and badgered till Tyler had told her they were Bella's and none of her business.

Which, of course, meant it became Marley Mae's urgent business to harangue Bella mercilessly till she could prise out a promise that when she *did* open them Marley Mae could help her.

And it seemed that time was now. When Lauren and I returned to the living room, now inhabited mostly by quietly playing kids and noisier slumbering men (Mike's snores alone could wake the dead), it was to meet Bella and Marley Mae coming out.

'We're going upstairs to open the presents,' Marley Mae informed us both before I even had a chance to ask. She was looking very pleased with herself.

'Oh, I see,' I said, clocking the way she had Bella's hand clamped in her own as if she were a prisoner who might abscond if left untethered. I looked at Bella. 'You doing okay, love?' I asked her.

She nodded, albeit wanly.

'She might have an iPodge!' Marley Mae added breathlessly, with the sort of awe a child of her age could feel for such wonders. 'Or even a *tablet*!' She was clearly very excited.

I wondered if I should gently prise her away and let Bella have some down time on her own. But when I suggested Bella might like five minutes' peace, it was Bella herself who responded. 'No, it's fine,' she said, and I could tell she meant it. Upon which, they both trotted off up the stairs.

'Don't you sometimes wonder,' Lauren reflected, as they disappeared out of sight across the landing, 'how little ones have no idea how much of a part they play in all this? Just think of all the foster children Marley Mae has befriended since she was born. Do you sometimes wonder if they ever think about her? You know, have memories of her, still? It's a nice thing to think that, don't you think? How, in all those children, there's a little permanent space in their brains where she lives? I love that as a concept, don't you?'

It was something I'd never thought about before, and I said so. 'Oh, but I *love* that,' I said. Because I really did.

They were up there a good while, and I resisted the urge to check on them, as did Riley. Even though both of us were ever conscious that the children who came to us began as strangers, we were of a mind, as was Lauren, that Bella posed no threat to anyone. Except, perhaps, to herself. Besides, the door had been left ajar and both Tyler and Mike had been upstairs since they'd gone up – and both had reported hearing Marley Mae giggling.

Still, once bitten, ever vigilant – and we'd certainly had our scares down the years. None of us would ever forget the day when Flip, a young girl we'd had with foetal alcohol syndrome, had taken it upon herself to give us a post-lunch break and take Marley Mae off for a walk in the local woods. So when over an hour had passed and neither had reappeared, Riley and I exchanged a 'Let's one of us just go and check what they're up to' expression. I was just rising from my chair – being the closest to the door – when my granddaughter marched in and made a beeline for the tree, below which her own sack of presents still sat.

'Oh, hello,' I said, glancing behind her to see no sign of Bella. 'So, what was the outcome? What did Bella get?'

I was rewarded by Marley Mae putting a finger to her lips and emitting the sort of self-defeating high-decibel 'Shhhh!' that was her trademark. 'She's going to *sleep*,' she whispered, falling to her chubby little knees to dig around among her haul.

'And she's sad about her mummy,' she added, turning around, having produced a cuddly toy; the cuddly snowman, from the film *Frozen*, that she'd been hoping for so much. 'So I'm going to let her borrow Olaf.'

Riley and I rose as one to go up with her, both first agreeing to the 'You must be quiet!' order she issued before agreeing to lead the way.

We trooped up, a little battalion, led by our diminutive general, and followed Marely Mae into Bella's bedroom through the now wide-open door.

And it was to find a room totally transformed. Everywhere – all over the carpet, the bed, and on any and every horizontal surface – was what looked like confetti, but made out of wrapping paper. Which I immediately recognised as the paper Bella's presents had been wrapped in. Only it had now been transformed into a million tiny pieces.

Bella herself appeared to be asleep. She was curled in an S shape, a tiny form on the bed, with both the rabbit we'd bought for her and her Dobby close beside her, while further down the bed was the 'iPodge' Marley Mae had been alluding to, together with other presents: some sort of nature annual, what looked like a folded hoodie, a pair of jeans and a jewellery-making kit.

'We torded it,' Bella whispered proudly, before tip-toeing theatrically across the carpet and gently placing her precious Olaf close by Bella's blonde curls. A holy trinity of stuffed animals to chase the nightmares away. 'There,' she mouthed silently, with admirable restraint, before turning back to us, placing a finger to her lips again and shooing us outside.

I pulled the door to, while Riley picked Marley Mae up, and as she now announced that she needed a wee we all trooped into the bathroom.

'You made all that confetti yourselves, did you?' I asked her, as Riley helped her with her pants.

'It's not confetti,' she told us. 'It's *snowflakes*. Bella liked making snow and she let me help her. I was *good* at it.' Then she frowned. 'But then she was sad,' she said. 'She cry-ded a *lot* when we were doing it. I tolded her you wouldn't be cross about the snow, Nanny, but she still cry-ded.'

'But I bet it looked pretty when you threw it everywhere,' Riley observed. 'And, oh, the joy of Hoovers,' she added to me drily.

I pictured the scene. Bella's distress. The emotional meltdown of seeing it laid bare. Of seeing it laid bare with an over-excited Marley Mae, who'd known no such devastation in her happy young life. Seeing the presents from parents who weren't with her – or each other – opened the gaping hole where the spirit of Christmas should be.

'Whose idea was it to make the snow?' I asked Marley Mae. 'Was it yours?'

She shook her head. 'Bella liked it.' She mimed a ripping motion. 'She likes making snow. And then she threwed it, like this –' She thrust her arms up and outwards. 'But she's sad now. She said. So I said I'd get Olaf for her to cuddle.' All done, she held her arms up for Riley to scoop her up again. 'You shouldn't cry on Christmas Day, should you, Mummy?'

I glanced in, as we passed, to our poor, anguished visitor, lost in dreams – good ones hopefully, *please* let them not be nightmares – beneath her blanket of multicoloured snow.

No, I thought sadly, you shouldn't.

Chapter 5

It's impossible to predict how a child will respond to extreme stress unless you know that child very well. And even then it's an inexact science. Even with more than two decades of mothering my own two under my belt, I could still find myself surprised by how they reacted in adversity, sometimes astonishing me by their fortitude and stoicism under pressure and other times collapsing under the strain of something apparently minor. Every one of us really is unique.

Which is why, with Bella, as with any child, I assumed nothing. Yes, I'd make assumptions about what she might or might not be feeling, but how those feelings played out in terms of how she coped with her current lot was something no one could predict. She also came to us without much back-story, which would have enabled us to get a better feel for her, and which was in contrast with several of the children we'd previously fostered, such as Justin (he of the bulging, six-year, thirty-failed-placements file) and little Georgie, who was autistic and had been in care, and therefore monitored, for almost all of his life.

Three days in, therefore (we were by now in the lull before New Year, the bedroom 'snow' gone and forgotten), and I felt almost as clueless about Bella's emotional make-up as I had when she'd arrived on Christmas Eve – the moving scene on Christmas night notwithstanding. She'd clearly got something out of her system, which was obviously going to be A Good Thing, but she'd spent almost all of Boxing Day – which was a quieter one, with the little ones gone, and the day lazier – withdrawn and uncommunicative. And though she'd come out with us on a trip to town, to have a nose around the German Christmas market, she'd simply done as asked, like a biddable elderly relation almost, putting her coat on, doing the buttons up, donning the gloves I'd found for her and then trailing along, hand in mine, but completely disengaged. The most animated she'd been was eating a doughnut. And she'd only managed to eat half of that.

Two days later, and she was still saying almost nothing to any of us bar Tyler, and what she did say – the odd 'yes', 'no' and 'thank you' – was always in response to something said to her. For much of the time, and I didn't push it, she had her nose in the Harry Potter book we'd given her. Reading, it was becoming clear, was her main refuge.

So today's masterplan (which wasn't any sort of masterplan, really; I was leaving that for John to organise once everyone was back in their various offices) was for the pair of us to go wedding-dress shopping with Riley, while her David stayed at home to mind the kids.

I had promised my eager-beaver daughter that I'd fit some time in in the New Year to go dress hunting, but with Mike back in work – to cover sickness; there'd been some grim virus going round – and Tyler off to spend the day with Denver, I figured today was as good as any to make a start, not only as it would stop the four walls of the silent house closing in, but also, despite the inevitably fraught nature of competitive sale shopping, it did mean we had at least a fighting chance (fighting being the operative word) of bagging a bargain. And since Mike and I were footing the bill, that would be a major bonus.

It was now 10 a.m., however, and though I'd been happy generally to let Bella sleep for as long as she needed to, given that Riley would be over soon, keen to hit town and do battle, it was probably time I went to wake her up.

And when I went upstairs I was pleased to find her bedroom door open; she'd obviously already woken up and gone to wash, though, in contrast to the previous three mornings, she'd left her duvet flung back and pillows awry. Perhaps evidence that she was finally beginning to settle, rather than carrying on as if in an institution, like her mother?

'Morning, love,' I called, seeing the bathroom door was also open, before heading off into my own bedroom to change.

I hadn't been expecting a response, but almost immediately I got one, though not in the form of words, more an anguished, groaning sob.

I backtracked to the bathroom and pushed the door properly open, to be confronted by an unexpected, shocking scene. Bella was sitting on the bathroom floor, her legs drawn up to her chest and her arms clenched around them, while, moaning softly, she rocked back and forth. And as she did so, because of where she was sitting, beside the toilet, the back of her head was drumming rhythmically against the sink.

Straight away I could see she wasn't doing it deliberately. Head-banging is a particularly distressing form of violent self-soothing so I was relieved to be able to see it wasn't that. She was simply oblivious, or, at least, not particularly concerned that the basin was in the way of her rocking. She certainly seemed out of it, like she'd gone into some kind of fugue.

And she clearly needed to be moved before she hurt herself. I bent down in front of her, which was when I noticed the vomit. There was sick all down her front, in her hair and on the carpet, as well as liberally decorating the bottom of the toilet seat and loo, the former presumably only having just been raised in time. How hadn't I heard all this? But perhaps it had happened while I'd been down in the conservatory, sorting the washing. Which meant she'd been here for quite a while. I cursed myself for not having checked on her since I'd come down at seven.

'Bella, love,' I said, automatically reaching to feel her forehead for a high temperature. 'What's wrong, sweetie? Do you feel ill?'

I pushed my hands under her armpits as I spoke, in order to help her up, and she raised her eyes to look at me in a way that made me realise she was only just becoming aware of her surroundings.

'Are you okay, lovey?' I said. 'You've been sick. Did you realise? Come on, let's get you off the floor and cleaned up.'

Again, I felt that same gentle compliance as I lifted her; felt the load drop a little as her legs took some of the strain, so I was at least able to release one arm to flip the toilet seat back down, and via a natty swivel place Bella back down on it, where she remained while I ran the tap and filled the washbasin with warm water and shower gel.

'I'm just going to wash your face, love, and wipe the sick up a bit,' I said, and when she nodded I found myself feeling slightly exasperated at her continuing inability – or was it determination – to communicate properly with any of us. Had she called out earlier – just that, just my name, so I could help her – she wouldn't be in this state now, would she? Not to mention my bathroom.

I quashed my resentful thoughts even as I had them. This was presumably why her previous carers had said they wouldn't have her back. And as they now had a brand new granddaughter, and all the anxiety and excitement that went with it, I could hardly blame them. They simply wouldn't have the emotional energy left to spare.

I had no such complications to excuse me. So, having elicited that she no longer felt ill, and that she didn't have a temperature, I dipped a flannel in the fragrant water, wrung it out and washed her down, making eye contact and willing her to respond to it. Which she sort of did, by way of heavy tears that sped down her newly cleaned cheeks – a picture of intense and perfect misery; ethereal, as if a character from a Victorian novel.

That job done, her hands dunked and dried, and her pyjama top wiped down, I helped her up and led her back into her bedroom. She needed to get out of her soiled pyjamas, obviously, but at twelve I hardly imagined she'd want me to help her with that, so instead I instructed her to strip them off and get dressed while I went back and sorted out the bathroom.

'If you want to have a shower and go back to bed, that's fine too, of course ...' But I had barely said the words when she became suddenly galvanised, crossing the room and flinging the duvet back over the bed, before furiously straightening it all out. It was almost as if she was terrified she'd get a slap if she didn't, and I filed the observation away for future reference.

'Don't worry about that,' I said, going across to her chest of drawers, where I pulled out a pair of jeans, a T-shirt and her new Christmas hoodie, which she had told me – on being asked – had been from her mum. Not her mum and dad, I noted. Just her mum. 'There you are, love,' I said, tossing them onto the bed. 'I'll go and sort the bathroom out while you get these on. And pop your pyjamas onto the landing for me to pop in the wash, will you? Then we'll try to find out what's made you sick, eh?'

I left her gingerly undoing the buttons on her wet pyjama top.

Back in the bathroom, I found myself in the unlikely position of ruing the fact that a day at the Christmas sales was probably a non-starter. Though logic told me Bella's sickness could have been down to a virus (in which case, the last thing I should do is allow it to be spread) instinct and experience told me otherwise. For one thing, though she had eaten extremely poorly since she'd been with us, she *had* eaten something the previous evening, and showed no signs of malaise afterwards, in the way viral tummy bugs tended to reveal themselves. We'd all eaten the same, too, and there'd been nothing in dinner that would make it likely that she'd succumbed to a bout of food poisoning.

No, instinct said she'd either been sick due to extreme distress and upset, or – a grimmer thought – that she had made herself so. Either way, given my responsibility to this distressed, highly anxious child, I needed both to log it and to consult our GP.

I was just wondering what sort of cover they'd have in the surgery, when I was stunned into stopping scrubbing by something entirely unexpected. A tiny but nevertheless clear voice.

'I'm so sorry, Casey.'

I swivelled around, on my knees, to find Bella standing in the doorway. She was dressed in the clothes I'd laid out on the bed for her, and in her arms was a bundle comprising not only her pyjamas, but also her duvet cover and sheet.

I stared long enough that Bella, tears once again streaming down her cheeks, came into the bathroom and stuffed the lot in the laundry basket.

'I wet the bed,' she said. 'I'm so sorry, Casey. I'll try not to do it again.' Her cheeks were crimson. She turned around and walked back out.

I sat back onto my heels for a moment and stared after her. It was really strange hearing her speak to me normally.

Speaking clearly, her head up, making eye contact, as opposed to her previous head-down, eyes-down, mumbling norm. And for some silly reason I fixated on the timbre of it – that it wasn't the high-pitched, tinkling little-girl voice I'd ascribed to her, given her muteness and her cherubic, baby-doll looks.

I got to my feet. She had communicated properly with me, finally. Not the biggest breakthrough ever – particularly given the icky circumstances – but a breakthrough nonetheless. Wetting the bed had driven her to speak to me properly at long last – which hadn't been *that* long, a matter of days, but, when a distressed child closes down, a matter of days feels a long time indeed. I clicked into gear, quickly wrung the cloth out and emptied the basin. The bathroom could wait. She was twelve years old, and she had wet the bed. And in a stranger's house. She must be feeling mortified.

I'd already heard her feet heading down the stairs, so I rattled down after her, finding her in the living room, curled up in her usual place on the sofa, and screwing the second bud of her new iPod into her ears, her eyes still damp but her tears having stopped now.

Oh no, missy, I thought, determined that we were not going to leave it there. I signalled for her to take the earbuds out again.

I sat down beside her. 'Bella, love, listen, please don't worry about the bed, okay? These things can happen, specially when you have been under a great deal of stress, and it's no bother at all to sort out. But listen, Bella, more important is that you've spoken properly to me finally.

And now you need to do so again. Sweetheart, do you have any idea why you might have been sick? I really need to call the doctor, you see ...'

'No!' She shook her head emphatically, making me worry once again that she might have made herself sick. 'Please no. I don't want to go to the doctor's. I'm fine. I don't feel sick any more, honestly.'

I shook my own head. 'Bella, you're not fine. How can you be? How could anyone in your circumstances?' I placed my palm against her forehead again, and she didn't pull away. She felt warm, but not hot. Stress and anxiety, I felt sure of it. 'Sweetheart, I have to register you with the doctor anyway, so he knows you're staying with us for a bit – that's the law. And I will just ask him if there are any nasty sickness bugs going around, okay? And I think we'll shelve the shopping plans today, give you a chance to rest and get your strength back.'

I stood up. I could see she was becoming anxious to retreat again, holding the earbuds in each hand, ready for reinsertion. 'And, you know, Bella, if you want to talk ... you must be keeping so much locked inside of you ... it might help. It probably would help – a problem shared and all that, you know? Anyway, I'm here, okay? Ready to listen.'

She didn't respond to that, so I thought I'd stick my neck out. What the hell. 'You must be missing your mum so much, Bella,' I continued. 'Not to mention worrying about your dad ...'

'Stepdad,' she immediately corrected.

'Sorry, sweetheart. *Stepdad*,' I said. 'Either way, you must be at sixes and sevens worrying about everything ...

so, I'm here, okay? Any time you need to get stuff off your chest.'

Again she shook her head. Again the action was emphatic. But then she surprised me by putting down both the earbuds and the iPod, uncrossing her legs and standing up as well.

'I should wash the bedding myself,' she said. 'Do you have a washing machine? I know how to work them.'

'Love, there's no need –' I began.

'I really want to,' she insisted, tears gathering in her eyes again. 'I've caused you so much trouble.'

I told her she'd done no such thing, but that it was fine if she wanted to, to go and fetch the washing, that I'd show her what to do. Genuine guilt, I wondered, or just a clever ruse to halt the whole 'talking' thing in its tracks?

As I watched her hurry back upstairs, I suspected both held equal sway. The time for talking was clearly not yet.

Chapter 6

I always feel a bit 'in limbo' between Christmas and New Year. I'm sure most people do to a certain extent. If you're in work, it often feels as if you're working in a ghost town, and if you're not, they are strange days, those short, end-of-the-year ones – all the Christmas bit – the whole gathering-of-the-clans bit – and then a lull before the next bit when the gathering happens again, which, like most people, I filled with shopping and re-stocking, scurrying round the house, catching up with missed chores and getting ready for the next round of visitors.

Bella threw herself into it too. While Tyler grabbed any opportunity to slip away and 'hang' with Denver, Bella, with nowhere to go and no one she could visit, seemed to have decided to keep herself occupied by doing housework as a competitive sport.

I wondered again about her home life and its apparently chaotic nature. About the alcoholic father and the impact it would have had on her. About how natural it was (and was so often witnessed) for a child who grew up with unpredictability the only constant to want to impose order and structure wherever they could. I wondered, given what I'd already heard about her parents, if she was something of a Snow White or Cinderella figure at home.

Not that her sudden interest in dusting meant a great deal more progress. Yes, she spoke a little more now, but only superficially about practical matters: 'Shall I put these in the airing cupboard?' 'Shall I do the drying up?' But never entering into territory that would involve talking about *her*. If I asked her anything personal she would immediately clam up. So I soon learned the best thing was not to try.

It was all a bit frustrating, this increasing attachment to the 'Christmas shutdown'. I felt reasonably happy that if there was any change in Bella's stepdad's condition – good or bad – I'd have been told. But I was anxious to get Bella help too. But though I'd been promised they'd seek a counsellor for Bella as a matter of urgency, I heard nothing till after New Year.

A quiet New Year, as it turned out, because though Bella hadn't succumbed to any further sickness Mike went down with whatever it was that had been rife at the warehouse – not badly, just a twenty-four-hour bout of gastric gymnastics – but enough to scupper our planned family party.

I was philosophical. It was almost as if it was meant to be. And though I dropped Tyler round to Riley's, where they were holding it instead now, I was actually perfectly happy in front of the telly, rather than doing my usual half hour with the *Radio Times* and the record button. I'd never admit it, but it was a novelty, and it actually made a pleasant change.

But when further news finally came, on 2 January, it was from John Fulshaw rather than Sophie.

It was dark, cold and miserable, as such days so often are, particularly so in this case, since I'd risen from my bed before seven, in order to do some online research on wedding flowers while Mike showered and got ready for work. Where my daughter was so chilled about everything that she was almost horizontal, I was fast approaching that mental place where 'There's still so much to *do*!' was my first and last thought every day. It comprised a good deal of the thoughts in between too.

The email from John had arrived in my inbox only minutes earlier and I half-decided to phone him and say, 'You too?' But then I decided if he was working that early the last thing he needed was me twittering on at him, so I settled down with my coffee and simply read it.

And it made for very interesting reading.

John obviously didn't have access to sensitive information regarding the case against Bella's mother, but he had been given access to the information about the family that the police had shared with social services.

Which was good news, and where multi-agency working really came into its own. Prior to the joys of the internet age, foster carers like Mike and me, not to mention a child's new school, and even their new doctor, in some cases, were kept largely out of the loop about their background. And even if this was mostly a sin of omission (though not in all cases; people could be very protective of the fruit of their own labours) it was almost always to the detriment of the child concerned.

Where, famously, an inability to cross-check and share information led to the infamous Yorkshire Ripper being arrested and let go an embarrassing number of times in the 1970s, there were countless far less high-profile cases, involving children in the care system, where information left unshared let them badly down.

So thank heavens for common sense and IT progress. It obviously made much more sense for everyone working towards the same end game to pool information and share what they knew – that way, all parties could work as a single team.

In this case, the report John had sent through about the family focused on one neighbour in particular. A widow in her late fifties, she was called Ellen Murphy, and had told police that she feared for Bella on many occasions, due to the volatile nature of her parents. They would regularly get into drunken brawls on a weekend, she'd said, and had, in fact, called and reported them more than once to the police, when she'd heard Bella screaming, thinking she might be under attack. She said that on every occasion (how many had there been, I wondered?) she had later been assured that Bella herself hadn't been in any danger – she'd merely been yelling at her parents to stop.

This had not, she said, lessened her fears. However much she'd been assured Bella wasn't in danger, she had personally witnessed the child lying out in the back garden, in the dark, often, and the cold, even the rain, drumming her feet on the ground, and covering her ears with her hands. 'I spent most weekends,' she'd added, 'with my finger poised over the dial button when it kicks off, just in case.'

Well, who wouldn't?

I was just thinking about the fine line between being a nosey neighbour and potentially protecting a vulnerable child (one I increasingly championed crossing), when the vulnerable child in question tapped me on the shoulder.

Thankfully, given the angle, I doubted she'd have seen anything I'd rather she didn't, but I quickly put the screen to sleep anyway.

'You're up early,' I said, then, following her gaze to the kitchen clock, corrected myself. Somehow, it was approaching 9 a.m. – something that seemed impossible till I remembered that at some point in my reading Mike had bent down, said 'Bye, love,' and kissed me on the cheek. I'd probably answered as well.

'Could I have a turn on the computer when you're finished?' she asked shyly, and I realised she held a pencil case and exercise book in her hand. 'It's just that if I'm not going back to school yet, I thought I could log into my homework page and do a bit of something to stop me being bored.'

Bella 'not going back to school yet' had been agreed before she'd even been delivered to us. With the likelihood of interviews, assessments, counselling sessions and the possibility of her even being moved out of county, it had been agreed that they should at least wait till the score was more properly known – a delicate way of describing the uncertainty about whether her mum would be charged with attempted murder or – please, no – just plain old murder.

And as nothing had happened to change that particular non-status quo (not to mention Bella having expressed no interest in going anyway) it seemed she'd be off for as long as it took.

'That's a good idea,' I said, popping the screen back to life briefly before quickly closing all the tabs I'd opened. And it was; the poor girl had only been in secondary school for a term when her world had collapsed, and a very short, no doubt fraught, term as well. I couldn't imagine how she must feel about that one constant in her life having been dramatically ripped away from her.

I hadn't made a start on Riley's flowers yet, but this was much more important. With Tyler on a last-night-of-freedom sleep-over at Denver's, I figured I could easily do that later. 'Here you go,' I said, pushing my chair back and inviting her to sit down. 'You get started while I go and make you some breakfast. Oh, and we have just the one rule about anyone who comes to us re the laptop, and it's that it has to be done here, I'm afraid. It's just one of those rules that we all have to follow. That okay?'

The 'here' in this case was, these days, a bureau-type unit that was part of our bigger 'entertainment' area. (Which now also housed the redundant karaoke machine, of course.) It was a bit cramped, but it was at least in a high-traffic area, which made it nigh-on impossible for anyone (should they want to – I hoped they didn't) to nose around in anything unsavoury. Needs must, in the fostering game.

'Oh, of course,' Bella said, as if it had never occurred to her that it might be otherwise. Which was refreshing; more and more it seemed teenagers treated laptops as extensions of themselves, to be operated *from* laps – ideally hidden from view, in their bedrooms. But this didn't seem to be the case with Bella, who, as far as I knew, had never owned a laptop – or else surely she'd have brought one along with her.

I left her to it and went to the kitchen to make some porridge with syrup – something (in fact the only thing) Bella had so far expressed a liking for. And while I stirred, I thought about the email I'd been reading and the picture I was building up of her family life before the 'crisis' – for want of a better word. I still felt unable to find the right one, since it was still unconfirmed – would it all too soon become Bella's stepfather's killing?

Whatever the future held, the past had clearly been a very unhappy place, and though she hadn't apparently been on the receiving end of physical violence, emotionally it must have scarred her quite profoundly. To witness violence and aggression on such a regular basis can't have made for a very happy life at all. And judging from the comments by the neighbour, Mrs Murphy, it was a crisis that was always going to happen.

The porridge made, I went back into the living room, to find the screen filled not with homework, but with flowers. Or homework *on* flowers, which was possible. And then I realised.

'I hope you don't mind,' she said, 'but I saw that your computer had a painting game on it, and I just thought I'd have a fiddle – I thought I might make a painting for my mum. Something I can take to her when they let me go and see her.'

It was the first time she had mentioned her mother since telling Marley Mae she missed her on Christmas night. She'd not once said the word 'mum' to me. Which I naturally didn't comment on.

'Oh, I *see*,' I said. 'I wondered what it was.' I leaned over her shoulder and peered closer. She'd done a great job; had produced a picture of a vase full of sunflowers that was obviously heavily inspired by van Gogh. But was still very much her own. She was obviously very creative. 'That's lovely!' I told her. 'Wow – I've never been able to manage anything like that on that app. Everything I've done has looked as though it was painted by a chimpanzee. A rubbish chimpanzee who's blind in one eye.' I got a little smile for that, which pleased me greatly. 'Do you know how to save it?' I went on. 'We can print it out. I'm sure your mum is going to *love* it.'

She saved the file (what was I like, trying to tell a twelve-year-old how to work a computer?), then turned and smiled again. 'They're her most favourite flowers in all the world. We planted some last summer – against the back wall of the house. And you should see them – they're so tall. Right up to the bathroom window.'

'Still?' I said, quietly astonished by this torrent of conversation. 'They're still there?'

Bella nodded. 'They're dead, but they're still there. All brown. We need to chop them down and get the seeds out of the flower-heads so we can grow some more ...'

Her face fell and I could see what she was thinking, because her thought was written all over it. 'And what about van Gogh?' I said quickly. 'Have you studied him in school?'

'We did him back in primary school,' she said. She sounded wistful. 'And Mum bought me the painting of the sunflowers for my bedroom.' She glanced back at the screen. 'I should have brought it with me, shouldn't I? Or had the lady go back for it. It's only little ...'

'You know, you could always do an image search and find it, and we could print that out as well. Then you could pin it up on your noticeboard, couldn't you? Anyway, porridge is ready, and you can carry on when you're finished. Fine art's every bit as good as school work, after all.'

Bella followed me into the kitchen and sat and ate her breakfast while I sorted a load of washing, wondering about the relationship between the two. Wondering about what kind of person Bella's mother might be. On the one hand a mother who's engaged enough to grow sunflowers with her daughter, to buy an art print, to be involved, and on the other a woman who brawled drunkenly with her husband in the street. People, I decided, were endlessly complex and fascinating, and no one could ever be second-guessed.

But there was still this little niggle. What sort of mother let her daughter witness such violence? She clearly loved Bella – well, I had no evidence that said she didn't – and surely a woman who cherished her daughter would want to protect her from witnessing all that she had? Surely she would rather leave her man than put up with that. Or was it a case – as I'd seen so many times – of love being blind? Of that endless hope that one day he would change? Much as it seemed Bella's mother was historically pretty feisty –

always giving as good as she got, which in some ways was good – was she also a hopeless romantic? Well, till the heartstrings he'd tugged on had snapped. Bella had mentioned a visit. Was there really any likelihood of that happening? I hoped so, but was pragmatic. I thought not.

It was the next day that I learned that if Adam Cummings himself hadn't exactly changed, his clinical prognosis finally had. He had been deemed out of danger, it seemed. So he was consequently off the ventilator, out of his drug-induced coma and, by all accounts, expected to make a recovery.

'A full one?' I asked John, who'd phoned telling me he had news, and who I phoned back once Bella was safely in the shower. Another day, and since Tyler was now back in school another attempt was to be made on the wedding-dress front. Time and Riley's nuptials waited for no one.

'Not clear,' John said. 'You know what it's like with head injuries. But sufficiently at this point to make a statement to the police, anyway. Of which the short version is that his wife attacked him without any provocation, and that he was sure it was with intent to do him serious harm. And the location of his major head wounds – which are at the back – would support that.'

I felt relief wash over me. So no murder or manslaughter charge, then. But this was still at odds with Bella's mother's 'self-defence' version of events, and, given the background of mutual violence, her defence lawyers would have a job on, as she could realistically still be looking at a charge of attempted murder, and a long prison term.

Sophie, Bella's social worker, called me soon after, to arrange the best time to come and fill Bella in, on both her father's condition and the severity of her mother's current situation; a task I was only too happy wasn't mine.

'I'd like to come later today, if at all possible, Casey,' Sophie told me. 'You know what it's like; walls have ears, the jungle drums, smoke signals and all that. The sooner she hears it from me, much the better.'

'Of course,' I said. 'Come tonight.'

Though I privately wondered – who on earth else was going to pass anything like this on to Bella?

Sophie was prompt enough – I think unfashionably early is the term – that when the doorbell went, Bella and Tyler were still eating their tea. And actually talking to each other, albeit mostly within the safe zone of Harry Potter.

Which left us ten minutes to sit in the living room and have a quick, private chat – though there was little to say that hadn't already been said, apart from Sophie's desire to have this particular task over with. I didn't blame her. It was good, certainly, that Bella's stepdad was finally off the critical list, but what he'd apparently told the police made her mother's situation one that was a great deal *more* critical. It also occurred to me that Bella herself, as a witness, could be asked to provide crucial evidence. Was she old enough to do that? Would they demand that she did? I suspected they could and, if necessary, would, whether it was by the counsel for the defence or the prosecution.

But first things first, which was to avoid discussing any such depressing matters by chatting away about how different a house looked after Christmas, specially one as bedecked as ours had been. 'I mean, seriously *blingtastic*. I couldn't get over it,' Sophie told me.

Her last appearance here felt like a lifetime ago. I said so.

'Tell me about it,' she said. 'My mum was *exactly* like you.' Which brought me up short – particularly the warm way she said it – because I'd got the impression that she had found it all a bit OTT and garish. She drove a very elegant BMW, after all.

'Was?' I said, her use of the past tense also hitting me like the proverbial sledge-hammer.

She nodded. 'It took me straight back. Honestly, for two pins, I could have moved right in along with Bella.' A pause. 'Seriously. We only lost her last spring. And you know what it's like. No one had the heart to do anything really. But I was, like – Mum would be *fuming* about this lack of effort! But in the end –' she shrugged. 'What with my case-load and everything, I didn't get around to doing anything either, so who am I to moan on at everyone else, eh?' It was only then that I noticed the raggedy edge around her smile, and remembered her relentless mega-wattage on Christmas Eve. 'Still, we got through it, me and dad. Sure it'll be better next year.'

My face must have given me away all too well. How young must this oh-so-young woman's mother have died? 'God,' she said, reading me. 'Honestly, it's *fine*, Casey. *Really*. Though I'm booking myself in here for next year. Okay?' And then she laughed.

And with consummate professionalism, as soon as Bella appeared from the kitchen she arranged her features for the tough job she now had to do.

It wasn't fine at all. But her mother would have been so proud of her.

Since I didn't take Bella finding her voice with us for granted, my main concern was that she'd clam up with Sophie. And as she came in there was no doubt she was anxious and wary – as well she might be; every single phone call and visit and email might have life-changing consequences for her. And she was old enough and bright enough to know that. She might be braced for the news that her stepfather had died, even – I'd been on strict instructions not to discuss anything about him at all.

Sophie put her at her ease straight away, though. 'Bella, I'm here mainly to bring you good news,' she began. 'Your stepdad's been taken out of the intensive care unit. He's still very poorly, but he's breathing on his own now and he's expected to recover well eventually. Isn't that good?'

Bella nodded. 'Thank you for letting me know,' she said stiffly. 'Does that mean my mum can come home now?'

I was watching her like a hawk, and was aware that Sophie was doing likewise. After all, Bella's testimony about what actually happened could now prove more important than ever.

I could see the way Bella's shoulders seemed to relax and how her demeanour subtly changed; from one of nervous anticipation, to one of relief. But now this key question. She was watching Sophie just as intently.

Sophie glanced at me. 'I'm afraid that isn't clear yet, Bella,' she said gently. Immediately Bella's demeanour changed again. She looked anxious, angry even.

'But you know what?' Sophie went on. 'You could go and visit your stepdad now, if you want to. You know, in hospital. Not on your own,' she added quickly, and I could see that, like me, she was trying to read Bella's expression. 'I'd be the one to take you, of course. I'm sure he'd be so pleased to –'

'Why would I want to go and visit *him*?' Bella said. 'If it wasn't for him, my mum wouldn't be in prison! My stepfather is a drunk,' she said then, and with such disgust that I think it took both of us aback. It was definitely the first time she'd come straight out and expressed a strong emotion about him. She sounded eerily adult. I could hear an echo, too. *Your stepfather is a drunk.*

'Sweetie –' Sophie began. Bella gave her a look that might just as well have said, 'Don't you "sweetie" me.'

'If he wasn't a drunk,' she pointed out, 'there wouldn't be all the fights. And if there weren't all the fights my mum wouldn't have had to do the thing she did, would she? To stop him killing *her*. Anyway, why not?'

'Why not what?' Sophie answered.

'Why can't my mum be let out of *prison*?' Her voice sounded more child-like again, not to mention wobbly. 'If he's going to be okay, then *why* can't she come home?'

Sophie seemed caught off balance by Bella's concise case history (which struck me as being spot on, in all probability; chaotic families so often shared the same sorry dynamic), and I wondered if she had already been directed as to how to answer her not unreasonable question. Would she be allowed to intimate that it was a question Bella herself could help answer, by telling the police what she'd seen? Apparently, yes.

'Sweetheart, I have to be honest with you about this. Yes, it's gr– um, *good* that your stepdad is going to be okay, isn't it?' She paused. Bella didn't even grace the comment with a nod, much less agree. 'But your mum still has a very serious charge against her. As things stand, she is going to be tried for' – another pause – 'attempting to kill your stepfather. It's very serious, Bella. Even though your mum says that's not the case, as you already know.' Yet another pause. Bella's eyes were locked onto Sophie's, as if held there by a tractor beam. 'Which is why it's now going to go to trial, and this is where you come in, sweetheart. Anything you can remember about that night is going to be vitally important. Any tiny little thing. I know you're scared to talk about it. I know it's probably very upsetting for you to even *think* about it, but … oh, sweetheart, don't. Come on. Don't cry … Come here.' She held her arms out. 'Come here,' she said again.

Bella brushed Sophie's arms aside, blind with tears now, and fled the room.

'So, that went well, then,' Sophie said, staring after her.

The bout of distressed tears was, thankfully, short-lived. By the time I'd seen Sophie out (after we both agreed it was only to be expected) and gone up to comfort Bella, her sobs had quieted to no more than the odd sniffle, and she was already sitting cross-legged on the bed, scouring her face with a tissue.

'I understand, love,' I told her, sitting down beside her. 'This must be all so distressing for you.' She sniffed agreement rather than answered, so I carried straight on. 'It's good news about your stepdad – there's that at least, isn't there? Or is that *not* good news, Bella?' I added on impulse, seeing the way her expression hardened. She let her features settle. A stupid question. She was hardly going to admit to me that she wished him dead, was she? 'But you know, as far as your mum's concerned, Bella, Sophie's right – you might be able to help her. Whatever you saw happen between them … you know, you can help her defence lawyers paint a better picture. Any little thing you remember. Anything they said. Anything your dad said to your mum –'

'Stepfather,' she said firmly. 'He's not my dad. He's my stepfather.'

'I know,' I said. 'Sorry. My mistake. But you know, Bella, if you –'

'I didn't see anything,' she said. 'Casey, I didn't *see* anything. Why do I have to keep saying the same thing over and over again? I didn't *see* anything!'

Except perhaps her mother, wielding a heavy object, hitting her stepfather. If I were Bella, in such a nightmare, would I have told on *my* mum?

I put my arm around her and she didn't try to wriggle herself free.

There was nothing to be said. No point in platitudes about it all working out okay. So I offered none.

'I know. Tough times, sweetie, eh?' I said, kissing her head. 'And I promise. No more questions, okay?'

* * *

Later that evening, with the kids in bed, and the spectre of Sophie's visit having taken itself off elsewhere, I decided to embark on a bit of soul-nourishing wedding shopping – favours and twiddly bits and fripperies and so forth – while Mike settled down to watch some road-rage programme that inexplicably mesmerised him.

And, straight away, I noticed that there were a whole load of tabs open, following Bella's belated homework session before she went to bed.

Except they seemed entirely unrelated to Key Stage 3, unless the syllabus had changed radically in the last couple of years. As I looked into Bella's browsing history, I could immediately see what she'd actually been doing, which seemed to have been taking a spin around English law. She'd searched 'criminal law', 'attempted murder', 'self-defence' and 'sentences', not to mention getting ahead of herself and also asking the search engine 'Is having a trial by jury best?' She'd also been on Facebook, which had my ears pricking immediately. Sophie had made it clear to her – she'd told us – that she'd told Bella she mustn't go on Facebook. Well, not mustn't so much, because she could really only advise her. Any mustn't would have to come from us, as part of any house rules. Which, of course, I'd never imagined I'd need to implement. Not with this child. But here she was, going on social media anyway. Perhaps she simply couldn't resist it. Perhaps she felt compelled to find out what was happening while she was holed up with us. But if so, who was she talking to? I wondered. And about what, and to what extent? If to any great one, then – to borrow Sophie's parlance – walls would most certainly have ears. And what, if anything, might she have put on her wall?

But as the log-in screen was blank, the fields not pre-populated, I realised it could have just as easily been Tyler on Facebook. Or even Mike, who had finally dipped his toe into social media and engaged with it at least three times a year.

'Well, what do you expect?' Mike said, when I dragged his attention away from the television to point Bella's possible activity out to him. 'You can't blame the kid for trying to find stuff out, can you? And re the Facebook, well, it'll have been all over the local papers anyway, wouldn't it? And her school will have said something about her absence, wouldn't they? Mind you, if she's got any sense, and she has seen things she wishes she hadn't, then perhaps now the itch has been scratched she'll leave all that alone for a bit. That's what I'd tell her when you speak to her tomorrow. Don't even go there.'

And in an ideal world Mike was absolutely right. In an ideal world we could take in our foster kids, wave a magic wand, and cut them off from all of it. All the discussion, all the gossip – no good ever came of listening to gossip. And more importantly, all the toxic relationships they had in their past lives. And I would tell her that, too, because these kids often didn't know what was best for them and would, given half a chance, particularly if seriously abused, sneak off, behind the wicked, nasty, child-stealing social's back, and send themselves right back into the hands of their abusers, who, so often, heartbreakingly, they still loved and missed.

Which was why social media was such a nightmare for social services and foster carers. How exactly did you stop any of that happening? Of the most vulnerable children, having been whisked to a place of safety, being tracked down by the very adults they had been enslaved and mistreated by?

No, not every kid had access to a home computer, but what the majority of children *did* have was their own smartphone, these days – sometimes children who didn't have a pair of shoes to their name, too. And even if you didn't allow them access to your wifi, they had pay-as-you-go contracts, with data allowances – a 3G connection, or some free wifi, and any child was good to go. And, since the dawn of the computer age, of log-ins and passwords, to places where it was hard for you to follow.

Still, I reassured myself, as I closed the laptop down for the night, at least none of that applied to Bella. No smart-phone, for one thing, so that was one less thing to worry about. And with her mum currently holed up at Her Majesty's pleasure, her worries were grounded not in the virtual, but the real world.

I checked myself, not being all-knowing. Or so I *hoped*.

Chapter 7

Bella's little spell searching the internet stayed on my mind all that evening, and was there again when I woke the next morning. It was obvious *why* she'd made the searches she did – those were all terms and concepts that would have been at the forefront of her mind since she was first placed in care. Someone, at some point – perhaps several different people – would have explained why she was in care and what the immediate future held for her; including the fact that what the immediate future held for her was really dependent on so many factors – and facts, or lack of them – that as things stood it was anyone's guess.

So it was a natural thing for her to do; specially given her obvious intelligence. But it was important that I alert Sophie Taylor right away – not least because it might have some bearing on what she'd seen.

'If nothing else,' I told Sophie when I got through to her (once again slipping the phone call in while Bella showered), 'it would seem to suggest she's aware of the gravity of the situation for her mother, wouldn't it? Which

76

suggests to me that she knows full well that she tried to kill her partner. That the "self-defence" plea isn't borne out by what she witnessed.'

'Perhaps I should have had more of a conversation with Bella about her mum,' Sophie mused. 'You obviously try to keep it light, to minimise their distress, but it looks like Bella's obviously old enough and motivated enough to consider worst-case scenarios, doesn't it? God, I *wish* she'd open up to us. I'm just afraid that what she might be reading could scare her even more. And, after all, none of us know what's going to happen to her mum now. Specially with what we're increasingly hearing.'

'Have you heard something new, then?' I asked, picking up on that immediately.

'Nothing specific,' she answered quickly. 'Just a general feeling that there's more to it than we know, that's all. I'm sure John will fill you in if anything concrete emerges.'

I quashed the urge to grill her further, knowing it would be inappropriate for her to pass on anything that wasn't cold, hard fact. 'Thank you,' I said instead. 'In the meantime, any progress with getting Bella that counselling appointment?'

It wasn't that I felt particularly optimistic that a counsellor would get anything more out of Bella than had been the case before she came to us, given her track record, but you had to do *something*. And with her not looking like going back to school any time soon, it was at least something constructive to help fill a day.

'Give me an hour,' she told me and, true to her word, she was back on the phone within the next one, with an appointment fixed for the following week, with a 'truly lovely' counsellor called Katie.

I told Bella, hoping she'd at least feel a little positive about it, rather than looking upon it as yet another sneaky way of getting her to say what she'd seen. I pointed out that she might find it helpful to have someone to share her feelings with, and that seeing a counsellor – particularly a truly lovely one – was one of the things we generally considered to be useful, since it was sometimes hard to express yourself to the people you were close to and that, since she lived with us, perhaps we might now fall into that category. Or people you weren't close to, but who you lived with, and so on. I pointed out that it might be good for her emotional health. Which obviously mattered as much as her physical health. And lots of other positive standard-issue stuff like that.

'I'm not going to talk to her,' Bella said.

I kept the faith, however, because counsellors could sometimes work wonders, and in the meantime I could only keep on doing what I was doing: giving Bella security and space. I also found the pen and paper I'd been meaning to, and encouraged her to write. It was another thing Sophie had talked to me about when she'd called.

'The first counselling session will be led by Bella herself,' she'd told me. 'No questions. Just a chance for Bella to talk about what *she* wants to talk about. Which, hopefully, will be her mother. Katie herself can only be open and honest about what we know as fact, of course. Which, as you know, isn't as yet a great deal. And won't be, I suppose, until Bella herself adds to what we know – or

her father does. I'm sure he's going to be formally interviewed by the police any day now, and it'll be interesting
to see what he has to say. She's not said anything about
him? About the fact that he's out of danger?'

'Not a word,' I said. 'And I've obviously not asked her.'
Since feeling her negative vibes whenever her stepdad was
mentioned, I had studiously avoided mentioning anything
more about it. In fact, as I suspected that to do so might
be to put strain on the tentative bonds we were beginning
to make with her. And the way she'd responded to the
news of his coming off the ventilator made me doubly
convinced that while she might not wish him dead (at least
not consciously), she didn't wish him well – her relief, I
felt, was much more about how the new situation affected
her mother than anything else.

'Of course,' Sophie said. 'And that's all the more reason
to encourage her to write to her mum. Letters vetted by
you, of course – you'll obviously have to make that clear to
her, as nothing will be allowed to get to her if it prejudices
the trial in any way. Or at least not to put them in an
envelope, so that we can read them first. Laura's solicitor
has been very clear that to protect her case there mustn't
be any reference to that night in the correspondence.'

I could see the sense in that, but I could also imagine
that that might be exactly what Bella wanted to talk to her
mum about, so I said as much.

'I realise that,' Sophie said, 'but it is what it is and we
have to follow those instructions, I'm afraid. It might
make it easier for Bella to accept if you let her know that
we are all trying to arrange a prison visit for her as soon as

possible. Now that Christmas is out of the way, we can get that sorted out pretty quickly, I reckon. Everyone back in the office, caseloads getting shifted onto the correct desks. But I'm probably teaching you to suck eggs,' she finished, laughing.

'Well, I *am* a grandmother,' I pointed out.

'I know! And of *four* grandkids – jeepers, I couldn't believe that when John told me.'

Flattery, in all likelihood, but it still went down well. I was warming to young Sophie more and more by the minute.

Despite Bella's negativity about it, the following Wednesday couldn't come too soon. It was now the second week in January and the new school term had well and truly kicked in, meaning Tyler was back in school, and doing all his usual after-school gadding about, and leaving Bella even more isolated than she already was.

It was really helpful, therefore, that she had taken as much to Marley Mae as Marley Mae had to Bella. It meant we could do lots of things with Riley – Marley Mae usually in tow, of course – including shopping, which Bella did seem to like, particularly when I told her we could buy some nice new clothes and toiletries for her.

She was also keen to get involved in the wedding preparations; she even helped Riley design the little name cards that would be placed on the tables at the reception so that guests knew where they would be sitting. This in itself was a boon because it gave me some time to myself, something I'd not managed to snatch since Christmas Eve, as Bella was increasingly becoming my shadow, in the way Marley

Mae liked to be hers – replacing fear and wariness with what almost felt like clinginess, in what seemed like a heartbeat. Understandable, I supposed, given we were on our own so much together, and a pertinent reminder of just how much she must be missing her own mum.

But not her stepdad. Again and again, everything seemed to point to that. And, at first glance, given his drinking and apparently well-documented violence towards her mother, this was perfectly understandable. But it definitely wasn't a given. I had personally looked after children who had monsters for fathers (and in one case a grandfather who was pure, undiluted evil) who had abused them horribly, but were still missed and cherished. And, to our knowledge, Bella's dad – or rather stepdad, but who had been around since she was very little – had never hurt her or abused her directly in any way.

Yet, when I went round to collect her from Riley's the following Tuesday afternoon, she told me something that seemed to suggest that where Bella was concerned he was the very opposite of cherished. Beside herself with excitement at the prospect of her own role in the forthcoming nuptials, Marley Mae had apparently asked Bella if she'd ever been a bridesmaid, and been responded to with a distinctly short (and uncharacteristic, at least where Marley Mae was concerned) 'no'.

Riley had then asked her, lightly, if she'd like to be one day and Bella had immediately begun to cry.

'Just like that,' Riley told me, while we were out of earshot in the kitchen. 'Eyes brimming, face screwed up – seriously distressed. I calmed her down okay, apologised, told her she mustn't cry – that no one would ever make her be or do anything she didn't want to. Upon which she howled even more, saying she'd *love* to be a bridesmaid, just not *ever* if her mum ever married him. As in *him*, properly spat out. There's seriously no love lost there, Mum, I can tell you. I know a lot's gone on, but you just get an instinct for these things, don't you? Anyway, it occurred to me that if she's still with you when we get married, we should give her a special role, shouldn't we? Give her a chance to dress up. Make her senior flower girl, or something.'

Bless my darling daughter, I thought, touched beyond words by her everyday, matter-of-fact, pragmatic kindness. 'You're an angel,' I told her, giving her a hug.

'I know!' she joked, brightly. 'Sometimes I even trip over my own halo, it's getting so big.' She spread her hands. 'Truth is, what else are you going to do with her? Put her in respite?'

I shook my head immediately. To ship Bella off into respite care over the very weekend she was as we spoke helping arrange – unthinkable. No, she'd be there, as she should be. I wasn't sentimental about things like that at the best of times, always smiling non-committally when friends showed me wedding pictures that were completely ruined by 'her ex' being in them. Or 'that old girlfriend he had who no one even liked', or because someone's cousin had brought along a child that hadn't been invited. It always tickled me, that. It was a record of a moment in time. That was how the day had been. It was life, not an artistic composition. Still, I supposed it was either a case of remembering uncherished memories, or the tendency people had to try and 'curate' their lives. 'That's what they do on Instagram, Mum,' Tyler had one day told me, very sagely.

'*Exactly*,' Riley said. 'Of course she'll be there. So since she'll be coming, she might as well make herself useful, mightn't she? Anyway, I haven't said anything, because I wanted to run it by you first. So I'll leave that job to you. Might cheer her up a little. Take her mind off her woes.'

But at the same time, reminding me just how desperate those woes were. And making me think of her mum, and the living hell she must be going through too.

There was good news on that front, however. Riley's suggestion about Bella being given her own special job at the wedding (as 'Marley Mae's official minder, more like' according to Mike, who thought it a decidedly shrewd move) was sufficient to galvanise Bella into writing to her mother, something which for three days I'd been unable to persuade her to do. It was almost as if it had given her something to write about that was far removed from the things closest to her heart. Which had struck me as strange in itself, given how close they seemed, but I wondered if my telling her that her letters would have to be read by her mum's warders had been sufficient to put her off the whole idea. In case she incriminated her mum inadvertently? I suspected so.

On Wednesday morning, however, in the hour before Katie the counsellor's arrival, she'd sat down at the dining room table and written at length. And, to add to the positivity I was beginning to feel about things, Sophie called too, to let me know that social services had just received a visiting order, allowing her to escort Bella to visit her mum in prison the following week.

'Honestly?' Bella asked, eyes wide, when I went in to tell her the good news.

'*Honestly!*' I parroted back at her. 'As if I'd joke about something like that, missy!'

At which she'd pushed her chair back, stood up and flung her arms around me. I hugged her back, glancing at the clock and realising that, with Katie due imminently, this really couldn't have come at a better time. She'd be in a much better frame of mind for her session than I could have dared to hope.

Katie herself was even nicer than I had dared to hope, too. The sort of warm, cushiony middle-aged woman you'd happily share your own problems with, too, such was the aura of kindness that she emanated, even if it was of the professional kind. As soon as she was over the threshold she gave Bella her smiling attention, refusing tea and coffee, and waving away my suggestion of biscuits with a pat of her stomach, and a cheerful 'Thanks, but this is what twenty years of biscuits have done to me already!'

I made them comfortable in the living room and dared to hope.

In the meantime, with both a coffee and two chocolate biscuits – shame to waste them now I'd opened the packet – I made my own base in the kitchen, to read Bella's letter, written in her small, artistic handwriting.

The Silent Witness

Dear Mum

Hi, it's just me, Bella, catching up with you. Are you okay? I hope you are well. I hope the food is edible. I am eating very well. I miss you LOTS.

I am seeing a counsellor today. Did they tell you that? That I have a counsellor? I'm supposed to tell her what I'm feeling about things, but I won't speak to her, Mum. I *won't*.

All I want is for you to come home. Casey and Mike and Tyler are really nice, but I miss you so much, Mum, I can't wait to see you. I think I find out this week when I can come and see you and I can't wait. Are you sure you're okay in there, Mum? Is it like a proper prison, like on the TV? I hope it's not, I hope it's a nice place. Don't worry about me, I am being really good I promise, and I won't talk to that lady who's coming. I will just get upset anyway.

I have some good news! Casey and Mike's daughter, Riley, is getting married and I've been helping her. Her little girl, Marley Mae (she is nearly four) is going to be bridesmaid. (There are three bridesmaids – Marley Mae, Dee Dee – who is Casey's son's baby daughter – and another cousin whose name I don't know. And two page boys, who are called Levi and Jackson, who are Riley's sons. They're nice too.) Anyway, if I'm still here – though I want to be home with you soooooo much ☹☹☹ – Casey has told me I am going to be like an extra bridesmaid, and will have a special dress and everything!

Anyway, I asked Casey and she said if you can come home before that, I can go anyway. Perhaps she would let you come too.

I have to go now but I love you to the moon and back. Hope to see you *very* very soon.

Your bestest friend forever,

Bella Boo xxxxxxxxxxx

That simple letter said such a lot about their relationship. It brought tears to my eyes, even when I read it for the second time, even though it didn't augur well for the session that was going on in the other room. You never knew; perhaps the subsequent news – that she now knew she would be seeing her mother – would make all the difference.

I put the letter down, slipping it under the flap of the envelope I'd given Bella for the purpose, which only needed to be addressed. To where, I wondered? I could only hope somewhere leafy and distinctly un-prison-like to look at. Her visit, depending on the way events unfolded, could haunt Bella for years to come.

I couldn't help but sigh, too. This was a mother and daughter who clearly loved each other very much, and it just didn't seem right that they might be *separated* for years to come. Could that really happen?

Get real, Casey, I thought. Of course it could. And, in truth, I didn't know how to feel. Deep down I understood that, whatever the circumstances, violence – particularly such devastating violence that it almost killed a man – was wrong and needed to be punished according to the law.

But, on the other hand, maybe Laura had been driven to a point where she completely lost control. Surely that would mean she couldn't be held fully responsible? Surely they couldn't convict her for attempted murder in that case? Surely they'd see it was self-defence, and, hopefully, acquit her? I didn't know – I didn't know the first thing about Laura Daniels, truth be told – but in my heart, whatever the legal outcome or the facts of her relationship with her partner, I somehow knew that this woman loved her daughter passionately. And their love, whatever happened, would endure.

In the short term, however, the counselling session didn't look like adding weight to Laura Daniels's cause. Once they'd finished, Bella went up to her room to attack some new schoolwork her school had sent in the post, so we could deal with the 'boring admin bits', as I put it.

'It was all very affable,' Katie said, once Bella was safely upstairs. 'She was a great deal more talkative than I'd expected, too.'

I explained that Bella was at least coming along well in that regard. 'But she said nothing of substance?'

Katie shook her head. 'I felt she was trying to please me,' she said. 'As if she knew what was required of her, but had already made her mind up that she had nothing to say to me. I believe she's been much the same in all her previous interviews. She spoke happily enough on safe topics: missing school, the upcoming wedding – congratulations to your daughter, by the way, you must be so excited! And how she enjoys playing with your little granddaughter, too, all of which seemed very genuine. But when I mentioned how much she must miss her mum, it was as if a shutter went down. Either that, or you have a lot of exciting goings-on just outside your living-room window. Has she opened up to you at all?'

I shook my head. 'She's just written a letter to her mum, at least, so that's good. And we heard about the visiting order just before you arrived, of course, which seemed to cheer her up no end.'

'Well, that was something she didn't even mention,' she said. 'So it's clear how it is. Still, it's only early days. At least we've met each other. It could all be different next time. When's she going?'

I didn't know, and said so, but in truth it wouldn't have been appropriate to say so even if I did. Though we were working together when it came to Bella, a counsellor such as Katie was a 'bought-in' service, so it would have been going against protocol to reveal anything to her that she didn't already know. It might seem silly, but with a serious court case ongoing, and several lives in the balance, protocol was king.

'Well,' she said, 'it looks like we might be in for the long haul with this one, doesn't it? So, early days. I'll speak to Sophie and hopefully see you again soon.'

'That would be great,' I said. 'I'm sure it's good for her, even if it doesn't produce anything her mother's defence lawyers can use.'

Katie frowned as she put on her coat. 'Well, you know my limitations in that regard, Casey. If Bella's made her mind up she's not going to say a single word about it, I'm the last person who's in a position to try and make her.

Though, in truth, in my admittedly short acquaintance with that young lady, I suspect there won't be *anyone* who can.'

I thought she was probably right.

Chapter 8

The prospect of finally seeing her mum transformed Bella. Not in the sense that it blew her cares away or made her excited – she was, if anything, extremely nervous about the impending trip – but it made her talk so much more than ever before.

Where she'd been adamant she had nothing to say about the incident to Katie or Sophie (and still was), within the sanctuary of the family it appeared we had finally gained her trust, because she talked at length about anything and everything – just as long as it wasn't about *the* thing, of course.

She fixated particularly about what she should wear. So on the Monday, after Mike had gone to work and Tyler had left for school, I took her into town and we chose a special outfit for her – a demure plum-coloured dress (even slightly old-fashioned, to my mind), and a pair of suede ankle boots to go with it. 'I can't believe someone gives you money so I can have these things,' she kept saying, when I explained that there was an allowance to make sure she had what she needed. 'Why? Why do *I* deserve them when so many children have nothing of their own? It doesn't make sense.'

I could have wept to think she truly believed she didn't deserve them. She, who had so little – and I wasn't thinking about material things, of course – and who was on the brink, perhaps, of losing even that.

On the Wednesday morning she was up early, washing her hair; we'd agreed that, again, once we had the house to ourselves I would do her hair for her with my 'posh' curling tongs.

'Mum won't recognise me,' she said, swishing her curls back and forth, smiling – even sounding happy, almost.

But it was fleeting. She was sad again, in an instant. 'I wonder what *she'll* look like,' she said, looking at me, wide-eyed, through the hand mirror. 'I'm a bit scared to see her, Casey.'

I switched the tongs off and bent to kiss the top of her head.

'Of course you are, sweetheart,' I told her. 'Who wouldn't be? And you're right to prepare yourself, because she probably will look different.'

'And in some horrible prison uniform, probably. I've seen them on TV.'

I shook my head. I was able to do so with confidence, having at least been able to establish that the prison where Laura Daniels was being kept was one with an own clothes policy. I wondered who'd taken charge of going to fetch those clothes for her. What, if anything, was currently happening at her home? Not to mention whether there'd be a chance to get more of Bella's things, should she want them – something I'd avoided discussing or even raising with Bella, since it would send such a strong message that her stay with us could be lengthy, and the spectre of her mum being found guilty.

'No uniform,' I told her. 'No ball and chain either, so don't worry. You know, you've never really told me what your mum looks like,' I went on. 'Has she got the same beautiful blonde hair as you?'

'Sort of,' she said. 'But she has to have her roots done. I take after my gran. Her gran was from Norway. She was a lady Viking.'

'Is that so?' I said, pleased and surprised by this observation. And also biting back my natural inclination to probe further – because this would be the gran into whose care she refused to be sent, and who, up to now, Bella had yet to even mention. It had been almost three weeks now, as well, since Bella had been with us, and not a word of communication from her grandmother either. Why hadn't she written to her granddaughter? Surely it would be the first thing she'd do? I made a mental note to suggest to Bella that she write to her gran, when she returned. I didn't know the circumstances and it would be wrong to second-guess them, but with the ordeal of a trial ahead, surely whatever bridges could be built should be? And she spoke about her gran now without rancour. Why *was* she so adamant she didn't want to go there?

'And you look like a princess,' I told her. 'There. You're done. Give us a twirl. Yes, you'll do.' I pulled the plug out of the wall. 'Don't want your mum thinking we're not taking care of you, do we?'

Which made her tears well up again, and I cursed myself – she was on such an emotional knife-edge – but she sniffed them back stoutly – crossly, even – and shook her head. 'No crying,' she said. 'Mum needs me to be strong for her.'

'Indeed she does,' I agreed.

'I know,' she said. 'Tyler told me. It's so sad about his mum, isn't it? I mean, his dead mum. Not you. He said we could maybe go and visit her grave one day. Did he tell you?'

I shook my head. 'But we can. If you'd like to.'

It seemed a strange kind of outing, but, then again, maybe not. Tyler's sense of self owed so much to the belief – which we'd always encouraged – that the best way for him to keep her close to his heart was to become the man she would have wanted him to be. I wondered what else the two of them had discussed. Bella smoothed her hands down her dress front. Matter of fact. Back in control. 'I think he'd like me to.'

'Then we'll go,' I said. 'Come on, princess. Let's get you downstairs. Sophie will be here any minute.'

Laura Daniels was being kept in a women's prison over a hundred miles away, so it would be a lengthy, four-hours-plus round trip, even in the sleek BMW.

We didn't linger on the doorstep as it was bitterly cold. I took Bella out to the car, wrapped up warmly in her thick winter coat, and she strapped herself into the front seat. At twelve she was deemed old enough to sit next to Sophie, and as they drove away I could see they were already chatting. I wondered if anything of consequence or of use to Bella's mum might be said. I hoped so.

I was just turning to go back in, to make a start on the housework, when I saw the postie round the corner of our street. He'd been with us for years now – he'd been doing the round since before we'd moved in, and as I recalled that he and his wife had gone on some sort of northern lights cruise over the holidays (a lifelong ambition) I was keen to hear how it had gone.

He waved – he probably had some post for me – and I waved back, so to be sociable I waited, rubbing my hands up and down my upper arms to keep them warm, while he delivered post to the two houses before me.

'At least it's not snowing,' he said, as he headed up our path. It was always some variant of the same cheery senti-ment. If it was gloomy he'd be pleased that at least it wasn't raining, if blowing a gale, at least it wasn't a tornado, and if raining at least it wasn't a monsoon. I wondered what kind of positive spin he'd put on it if he was delivering post in an Arctic blizzard. But I didn't doubt he would.

'I wouldn't mind some snow,' I told him. 'Cheer the place up a bit. So, how was it?'

'Bloody parky!' he said. 'I don't think I've ever been so cold. Me! Feeling the cold. Would you credit it? But it was in-*cred*-ible,' he enthused, then spent what was obviously an enjoyable five minutes telling me all about it, while the cold January air whistled round my dressing gown and made it billow round my legs.

I agreed that Mike and I would put it on our bucket list as I took the post from him, and it wasn't till I was back indoors and riffling through the half dozen depressing post-Christmas bills that I realised one of them was hand-addressed – these days a rarity – and, moreover, in an unfamiliar hand.

The envelope was cream, the handwriting sprawling and slightly childish, and moreover it was addressed just to 'Mrs Watson', and minus a house number or a postcode.

Which was odd in itself, I thought, as I lifted the kettle, felt the weight, put it back and slapped the switch on. But perhaps it was from one of my former pupils, I reasoned. I'd spent a few years working as a behaviour manager at the local comprehensive, and I got the odd letter from my former charges from time to time.

Which would be nice, I thought, making my coffee and sneaking one of the remaining chocolate biscuits, before settling down at the kitchen table to have a read.

As letters went, it was already something of a disappointment when I pulled it from the envelope, which had obviously been deceptively thick. It was a single sheet, with writing on only one side, the inside. I unfolded it, and started to read.

Mrs Watson
You don't know me, but I know you have Bella Daniels living with you, and I'm a concerned citizen.
[Concerned citizen? What did that mean when it was at home?] I don't know what you have been told, but I've heard that you are making waves and jumping to conclusions about what happened with her parents. I

say parents, but actually, Adam is only a stepfather, a very good one I should add!

What? I thought. Making waves? Jumping to conclusions? Since when? I read on:

> I suggest that you step away from this and *keep your nose out*. You have no idea what really went on that night and what led to it. Ms Daniels (Laura) isn't as innocent as she would have people believe and there are two sides to every story. I suggest you take my advice very seriously!
> Yours, a concerned citizen. [Again.]

To say I was gobsmacked would be an accurate description of my expression when I finished reading, as I was definitely open-mouthed. What a cheek! And who was this? A neighbour of Bella's parents? The outspoken Mrs Murphy? A friend?

I picked up the envelope again, a worm of anxiety growing. It was correctly addressed, in terms of the road at least, and bore a festive Christmas stamp. Whoever it was knew where we lived. Knew where *Bella* was, which was worrying in the extreme.

I needed to get straight on the phone and ring John Fulshaw. I had to report this as, no matter how you tried to dress it up, it was also a very thinly veiled threat.

Chapter 9

It was a good thing that the prison was so far away as I had more of a fight on my hands than I'd imagined. I knew there were protocols for when a child's location was discovered, but had thought some sort of investigation would be in order as a next step, not the knee-jerk reaction I was hearing.

But the evidence of my ears was incontrovertible. John Fulshaw was telling me the next step was clear – putting plans in place to remove Bella from us as soon as possible.

'What? *Why?*' I spluttered, unprepared for him taking such a radical stance. 'No, John, *please*. We don't need to do that. It was just a crank letter! It could be from anyone.'

'An "anyone" who just happens to know your address,' John pointed out. 'Come on, Casey, you know as well as I do that a carer's information is kept strictly confidential. This could be a potentially dangerous position for you. I mean we are possibly talking about attempted murder charges here, don't forget. This isn't your regular "parents are fighting" situation. Not by a long shot. The stakes couldn't be higher.'

'I know that,' I conceded, the reality and gravity of the situation finally beginning to properly hit me. 'But surely we don't have to give Bella up just yet. Can't we – you, someone – do a bit of digging first? See if we can find out who it might be? From the writing it looks like it could be another kid, even. Oh, please, John. Seriously. Let us hang onto her for now, please? Leaving us, particularly now, would definitely set her back.'

The line went silent for several seconds and I knew John's mind was ticking away as he thought about the best course of action. A course of action, no doubt, that he felt would both keep me happy and all of us, myself and Mike included, safe.

'So how do you think this happened, Casey?' he asked me, after what seemed ages. 'How do *you* think someone got hold of your address?'

I had been racking my brains with the very same question, and had come up with only one possible answer. 'Well, it has to have come from Bella herself, obviously,' I said. 'Tyler has been with us long enough to know all about confidentiality, so he certainly wouldn't have been blabbing about it at school or anywhere, though I will obviously ask him just to be sure. Not that his circle of friends and Bella's would even overlap. No, I think Bella must have told someone, mustn't she?'

I hadn't mentioned that first time when it occurred to me that she might have gone on Facebook, and I didn't now. But I also thought back to the nights when I'd allowed her on my laptop to do her homework, and immediately felt stupid for trusting that's what she was doing.

No, she'd not talked to us about any close friend up to now, but that didn't mean she didn't have them. Or, indeed, want to make contact with them. 'She could have been chatting to friends online,' I admitted sheepishly, feeling like I was in a headmaster's office. 'She's not been going to school, has she? Which has obviously isolated her from social contact, so it's probably been naïve of me to assume all she's been doing on the laptop is visiting her school website and a bunch of educational sites. I've been lax is the bottom line, John. This is all *my* fault, probably. I began by watching her like a hawk, but you know how it is …'

I heard something like a splutter from the end of the line. 'If you think that "all *my* fault" line is going to soften me up, Casey, you're wrong,' John said sternly. 'And it's certainly not your fault anyway. You're not expected to be hovering over her shoulder every moment of every day, and she's almost a teenager, so of *course* she'd want to reconnect with her friends. Yes, I imagine that'll be what's happened. Okay, so here's what I propose. Ask her. Let's see if that is what's happened here. A worthwhile discussion anyway, as she obviously needs to know how important confidentiality is – that she must not divulge her whereabouts to even her closest friends.'

Relieved beyond measure that no one was going to swoop in and whisk Bella away, I agreed to do just that, and assured John that I'd be more careful in the future. In truth it was my fault, whatever he'd said. No, I wasn't expected to hover over her like the proverbial 'helicopter parent', but I should have been more savvy, and mentioned security to her every flipping time she used the computer. Kept at it till it had sunk in. Not blithely assumed that because she acted like she had no one in the world – she hadn't mentioned a single friend to us, after all – she didn't have a whole bunch of them she wanted to chat to. Stupid, stupid me.

We also decided that, though John would have to report the letter to both social services and the police, we would be better not mentioning it to Bella just yet. There was no point in worrying her further if we didn't need to. And the last thing I wanted was to dampen her good spirits the minute she returned after her long-awaited visit with her mum.

No, I wouldn't mention the letter yet, but I did need to address the situation because John was right about one thing for sure. On no account did we want our address bandied about in cyberspace for anyone to see. Bella herself was obviously only a part of the picture. We'd been fostering a long time, and looked after children from all sorts of scary backgrounds. I dreaded to think who else might now know exactly where we lived.

That's the thing about fostering. It never ceases to bring you up short and confront your preconceptions. Not to mention keeping you on your toes. Even though you are doing your best for a child, and in most cases trying to work to get them into a better place with their parents, so that, if possible, they could be returned to them, some parents didn't see it like that.

For some parents – and, sadly, it was often the least able and responsible parents who responded to intervention like this – we weren't helping at all. No, we were either misguided do-gooders, or meddlesome professionals with ulterior motives, who were interfering in their lives and being pivotal in tearing their families apart. Which is why I have the utmost respect for social workers; they are truly on the front line of what very often feels like a war zone.

It's also the reason why children have sometimes been placed into care and the parents are often not told where their children are. But in our modern world, it's no longer as simple as that, and, of course, older children, these days so 'social media-savvy', aren't stupid. Also, in cases where unsupervised contact is permitted, you'd have to be pretty naïve not to realise that if a child wanted to they could just *tell* their parent where they now lived. That said, if unsupervised contact is on the table, it's invariably because things are moving towards reunion, and the mum or dad are well aware that they must never use that information to turn up at a foster carer's house unless invited.

Over the years Mike and I have had many parents come to us, in fact; usually for their annual or twice-yearly LAC (looked-after child) review, which is mandatory for all children in care. But the thought of someone lurking in the neighbourhood, possibly watching what we were up to, was never going to be anything but worrying.

But for the moment we had a stay of execution, at least, and for what it was worth (which was probably little, given my silly laptop blunder) I didn't think our 'concerned citizen' posed any real threat. No, it seemed obvious it was just someone fighting Adam Cummings's corner; perhaps a nosy neighbour who was batting for his team. And why should I assume I knew better? Perhaps Bella's mum *was* guilty of whatever she'd been accused of. I'd never met her, and from what I did know about her (giving as good as she'd got – all that fighting – was a theme that had been established early) it was all entirely possible.

It was also not my concern and none of my business. My job was simple: to keep Bella safe and well. And with a couple of hours still before I had to return to that particular duty, I decided to blow away the cobwebs and the jitters by doing a round trip of my own kids.

I fetched up at Kieron and Lauren's first – Kieron worked all sorts of odd shifts, so could sometimes be found at home on a weekday – happy to spend an hour in the company of my youngest (and gorgeous, naturally) grand-child, little Dee Dee. She was going to be two in March, only a week or so after the wedding, but Kieron and Lauren had sensibly kept me out of the planning for that particular soirée, busy as I was with the ones for what he'd taken to calling the Wedding of the Century – ever the enthusiast when it came to winding his sister up. 'And that's with ninety-odd years of the century *still to go*, remember,' he always added, drily. And usually got a slap for his trouble, too.

It was good to flop down on their big squashy sofa and relax, with a ticklish granddaughter giggling on my knee. Though not for long; the 'baby' was a long way from babyhood now, of course, confident at walking and as prolific a chatterbox as my other granddaughter was. What was it about the girls in our family? I often wondered that. Till Riley reminded me – as she invariably did. 'Er, looked in the mirror lately, Mum?'

'I'm sorry we haven't been round these past couple of weeks, Mum,' Kieron said, smiling as Dee Dee wriggled and writhed under my onslaught of tickles. 'But with you having your hands full with Bella, and our Riley taking up all your free time, we thought it best to let things calm down a bit.'

'Oh it's fine, love,' I said, touched at Kieron's pragmatic assessment of the situation. 'Though in truth, with Bella not up to going back to school yet, I've been a little bit stir crazy. Still, seeing her mum today will hopefully be a big boost to her spirits. Perhaps she'll even feel like testing the waters.'

'That's no small thing, is it?' Lauren mused. 'You know, school. She must have only just found her feet at her own high school, mustn't she? So the thought of having to be the newbie at a completely new one … scary. I suppose there's no chance of her going back to hers in the short term, is there?'

I shook my head. 'Much too far away, particularly as this is all so open ended. Who knows where she might end up, if her mum goes to prison. My hunch is it's not going to be with her stepdad. No, scrub that. There's no way it'll be with her stepdad. So if her mum does get a prison term, who knows?'

'You can't even imagine it, can you?' Kieron said. 'You know, your mum being sent to prison. Being sent away to live with strangers, knowing they're locked up. Doesn't even bear thinking about …'

'So *don't* think about it,' Lauren told him firmly. She knew my son and his sensitive nature oh so well. 'Anyway, listen, Casey, in the short term, d'you think she'd like to come along to my dance class? Now Dee has a nursery place, I'm starting them up again, part time, straight after the wedding. I just confirmed the hall rental this morning, as it happens.'

Lauren was a beautiful, classically trained dancer and had run popular local dance classes locally for several years now. From toddlers to teenagers, she instilled grace in them all. Our last long-term foster child, Adrianna, had benefited from them hugely, though in her case, as she was an older teenager, and a dancer herself, more from passing on her own talent, and helping Lauren out, than having lessons.

Either way, Bella seemed a graceful girl too, and I thought she'd probably enjoy it. 'That would be brilliant,' I said, mentally crossing my fingers that we'd still have her with us at that point; that she wouldn't be dragged off to start again with a whole new foster family. Because one thing was for sure. She wasn't going home to her own family any time soon.

Having come away from Kieron's, I then quickly popped into Riley's, though as she had a couple of her friends round (and, of course, their own selection of manic pre-schoolers) I only stayed long enough to be given the latest to-do list, including such fine-tuning details as 'Ask Father Brennan if he'll make sure to remember to put the heating on *at least an hour* before the service!'

That was my daughter, I thought, the delegating supremo. She knew as well as I did that getting Father Brennan to move his thermostat would require almost as big a miracle as Moses being able to part the Red Sea.

Smiling to myself, I pocketed the list, wondering if Mike putting a solar panel on the church steeple might be the easier option. I then hurried home to wait for Sophie and Bella, feeling hopeful. Seeing her mum could – would – surely work wonders.

It hadn't. I could tell that the very moment I saw Sophie's expression. And then again, more clearly, as they came up the path, and Bella, her face tear stained, gave me a wan look by way of greeting and headed straight up to her bedroom.

I could also tell by the look of defeat on Sophie's face.

'Not good then?' I asked quietly as I ushered her into the living room.

'Not quite what we expected,' she said, shaking her head. I asked her if she wanted a coffee and she nodded, slipping her coat from her shoulders. 'It was all just a bit weird, to be honest,' she said. Here,' she added, as I turned to head into the kitchen to get the drinks for us, 'let me come with you and help you, so we can chat.'

She followed me into the kitchen, drawing the door almost closed behind her. 'Casey, it was *so* weird,' she said again. 'They were both so uncomfortable. You know, seriously odd together, and not just the usual stiffness because you've got this great fat social worker stomping all over your privacy –' she said, grimacing. 'You know what it's like … But weird with each *other*. Like they couldn't find

105

a single thing to talk about. Really strained, like they were both searching for mundane topics of conversation they could talk about, while having a completely different conversation with their eyes.'

'I'm sure it must have been because you were there,' I mused. 'And perhaps not strange at all, given how Bella's been so consistent in not saying anything about that day. You were there. Subject off-limits. Don't you think? God,' I said, 'and how they must want to talk about it. And *need* to. Must be like a ticking bomb for both of them. Well, I say both – we've no idea what her mother's told the police, have we? Or how much it differs from her partner's version of events. But as far as Bella's concerned … I mean, as a mother myself, I can completely understand how awful Laura must feel and how desperate she must be to explain her actions to Bella. Talk her through it. Help her make sense of what she witnessed. Truly awful position to be in, don't you think?'

Sophie sighed. I knew she was struggling as much as I was with trying to reconcile the legalities of the situation – a probable charge of attempted murder – with the reality of how it *really* might have been. She was a social worker, and I was a foster carer. We both knew how women in challenging relationships were often powerless to escape them, either financially or emotionally and, as a result, were very often pushed to breaking point.

'What was she like, anyway? Bella's mum?' I asked.

'Thin,' Sophie said. 'Gaunt, in fact. Same eyes as Bella. If I had to choose one word to describe her, I'd say haunted.'

The coffees made, my next job was to ruin Sophie's day further by imparting the news about the letter – something I'd promised John when we'd rung off earlier, since I'd be the one to speak to her first.

She groaned. 'Good grief! So are we removing Bella, then?'

I shook my head. 'Not yet. That was John's first thought, obviously. But I asked him – no, begged him – to reconsider. The risk just doesn't seem to warrant such drastic action. Not to my mind. The way I see it, if the threat was real then it wouldn't be just a warning note, would it?'

I gave Sophie the letter. She read it and digested what I'd said. 'I take your point,' she said. 'Still, my line manager might not see it like that. She might decide that it's absolutely in Bella's best interests to move her. It's not good if people with a grudge know exactly where she is, is it?'

'I know,' I admitted. 'But I'm really not seeing it. I don't think there's any threat towards Bella herself in all this.'

Sophie smiled at me over her mug. 'So just towards you and Mike, then? So – phew – that's all right.'

For all that the idea of Mike taking on all comers was amusing, none of this was really funny in the least. I was actually quite surprised by how seriously those in charge seemed to be taking this – did they know something we didn't?

Before Sophie left, I reiterated what I'd said to John about getting to the bottom of the leak. Perhaps if I could trace it back to a specific source they'd be in more of a position to assess the level of threat. I also wondered if all my years in fostering had hardened me up to real life, to an extent that while I was obviously concerned that our location might be out there, I no longer saw threats such as this as something to be lie-awake-at-night afraid of. I'd only been half joking with Sophie, truth be known. I really did think Mike could see off anyone who dared to threaten us.

Which was clearly insane, I chastised myself, as I waved Sophie off. We didn't have a clue who we were dealing with. Which meant my next job (and before Tyler got home from football practice, ideally) was to tackle Bella about it. Though after the emotional day she'd had, I didn't hold out much hope of getting to the bottom of things.

As it was, when I went up to Bella's room the poor girl was far too upset to even speak. It took a long period of hugging her and stroking her to even still her racking sobs.

'It was *awful*, Casey,' she told me, still crying freely, once she was calm enough to speak. 'It was so old and dirty, and so *cold*, and Mum looked so *thin*. And so scared. She kept looking round all the time, you know? Like she had the jitters. Like she was waiting for someone to pounce on her or something. Do you think that happens in her prison? People attacking people, people fighting? I can't bear it. I didn't know what to say to her. What could I say to her? I just want to make it better.' Her shoulders heaved again. 'I just want them to let her come *home*!'

'It's okay, baby,' I soothed. 'And I'm sure she's safe. No, I *know* she is. She won't have anything to do with any bad people, I promise you. She'll be in a special part of the prison. A less "prison-y" part, if you like, where she's safe. They'll be sure to take care of her and protect her. That's their job. And of course she's thin. She's been through a terrible time, just like you have. You found it hard to eat when you first got here, didn't you? Were sick and everything … Well, it's just the same for your mum. She'll be coping. She'll be strong for you … And everything will work out … it *will* get better, I promise.'

I stopped myself there. Who was I to be so bloody optimistic? For all I knew, things would work out really badly, and I felt even surer that the thing that was driving all this misery was that Bella knew exactly what she had witnessed that day. And her mother knew exactly what she'd done that day, too. What was the saying? That the devil was in the detail? Well, the devil here was the business of trying to decide if she'd been pushed beyond reason by the man she'd attacked. That the attack really was self-defence.

But the truth was that I *should* be optimistic with Bella. There would come a point in the future when things *would* get better. That was how life generally panned out. She might have a stormy sea to navigate before that, but, one day, her life *would* be better than it was now, wherever these events meant life ended up taking her.

'But how?' Bella cried, sobbing louder than ever. 'How will anything ever be the same again? Why did Mum have to tell them what she did?'

'Because it was the right thing to do, love,' I said. 'It's always right to tell the truth, whatever the consequences you have to face. She'd have been in more trouble if she'd have lied about it, wouldn't she?'

Bella took this in, and it occurred to me that now might be the time to ask her the question I wanted to ask about social media, but she surprised me by pulling away from me and flinging herself face down onto the bed, her little fists pummelling the duvet at either side of her.

I had clearly hit a nerve. I rubbed her back and, after a time, she stopped shaking and rolled onto her side. She pulled her legs up, and I took her ankles and rested them in my lap.

'Casey,' she said quietly, 'is it ever right to tell lies?'

'That's a hard one to answer,' I told her, ears pricked with anticipation, running with wherever she was about to take me. 'But, off the top of my head, I'd say there will be the odd occasion where it's the right thing to do. A white lie, for instance, to cheer someone up, or not to upset them. I remember Riley once coming back from the hairdressers having had all her hair cut off, and she hated it, and regretted it bitterly, and cried and cried and cried, and I told her she looked lovely every day for days and days, even though I hated it too. Because there was nothing she could do, was there? They couldn't stick it back on. And then, well, it grew a bit and we both got used to it.'

Bella slipped her hands under her cheek. 'But a big lie?'

'Have you told a big lie, then, Bella? Is that it?' I stroked her back again. 'Something you want to tell me about?'

She chewed her bottom lip for a long time before speaking. Was she about to recount what she'd witnessed at long last? The silence stretched. 'Because you can, you know,' I added eventually. 'If you want to. If you think it'll help.'

She shook her head then, and I wasn't sure how to respond. Did I ask her if the headshake was because she hadn't told a lie, or if she had but had opted not to share it?

'It's okay, love,' I said, conscious that to press her would be inappropriate. I must never lead. Only listen. That particular fostering edict was, rightly, set in stone. Instead, I returned to the currently pressing matter of our address being known.

'Sweetheart, listen,' I said, after she'd stared into the middle distance for so long that it was almost as if she'd forgotten I was there. (If this had been a moment, then it had, for the moment, passed.)

She turned her gaze back on me. 'Have you been chatting to friends on Facebook?' I asked.

Her answering nod was instant. Something else that had been weighing heavily?

Another pause, then: 'You know last week, when you came up and asked me how the geography project I was researching was going? I hadn't been doing it. I'd been on Facebook, even though I knew I wasn't allowed to.' I remained silent. 'I just *so* wanted to speak to my best friend,' she finished.

Her best friend. She'd been almost a month with us now and this had finally been acknowledged.

'What's her name?' I asked.

'Ruby.'

'Ruby and Bella,' I said. 'Two lovely names together. You must miss seeing her. And her you. Have you been friends a long time or did you meet at high school?'

'Since I was eight,' she said. 'When she came to my primary school. She doesn't go to my high school. I wish she did.' Bella's chin wobbled. 'She hates her new school. I miss us going to the library together. That's what we did lots, at the weekends. Everyone calls us both geeks.'

'Well they're idiots,' I said firmly. 'And what utter nonsense. Don't they realise? Libraries are one of the cornerstones of a civilised society. I read that somewhere,' I added. 'Probably in a library book, come to think about it ...'

This elicited a ghost of a smile. I decided to seize this new moment. All these moments were still steps on the longer journey, after all. 'Listen, sweetheart,' I said. 'I'm not cross about Facebook. You know you did wrong, and that's good enough for me. And you know, as long as you don't put our address on it – same as with your mum – you can write a letter to Ruby, too – every day, if you like. And she can write back to you, care of social services. But listen, love, might you have accidentally told Ruby where you're staying? You know, have you told her our address?'

She lay still for a moment, then screwed up her eyes. 'I did ...' she said, finally. 'Oh, God, I'm sorry, Casey. I did. We were just chatting ...'

'What, in a private message?' I asked hopefully.

She frowned. 'No, on her timeline, under a comment. Just under a comment to each other, not on the main thread, to everyone ... so it's not like people would see it automatically or anything ... but ... oh, I'm such an *idiot*.'

She might as well have been speaking to me in Finnish. 'But her friends *could* still see it ...'

'Yes, but not properly. Not without clicking on the "replies" button. Oh, God, I'm *so* sorry. She was just asking how far away I was.' She heaved herself back up to a sitting position. 'And I only said your road … not your number – I didn't even remember the number, so I wouldn't have done. It was only because her auntie lives round here, that's all … and she thought she might know it …' She wiped her eyes against the backs of her hands. 'Why? Does it matter? I can delete it all. I can do that straight away. I'm so sorry. I thought you'd be cross because I was looking at all the horrible things people have been saying … I didn't think it was –'

'Have they?'

She nodded miserably. 'About my mum. And my dad, too. But mostly my *mum*. I *hate* them. They don't know *anything*!'

Antennae all a-twitch now, I reached out to comfort her. 'Hey, hey,' I said, drawing her to me again. 'Let's not even given them a second thought. You're quite right. What do *they* know? Nothing. About *anything*. Which is *exactly* why they are best ignored.'

And because I could sense we had arrived at a new level of openness, I decided to back-track a little, for fear of saying something that might slam the door shut again.

'Listen,' I said again. 'Let's just sort out what we can. You know, you putting where you're staying up on Ruby's Facebook. Let's get that sorted, eh? And you know, it's not even about *you*. It's just that Mike and I have to be very, very careful about things like that – about who knows where we live. Because of all the other children we look after, it has to be kept private.'

Bella nodded and sniffed. 'Well, if I go back on I can delete it all right now. Would that help?' she asked.

'Absolutely,' I said, rising from the bed and holding out my hand. 'And maybe you could message Ruby and explain you'll write to her – the old-fashioned way – instead. Come on, kiddo,' I said, 'let's go and do some damage limitation, then, shall we?'

The question, of course, was where the damage had been done. Who had seen what. Who had decided what. Who had said what. What network of connections flowed out from those timelines. What wider feeling was prevalent re Bella's parents. *Mostly about my mum*, Bella had said, re all the vitriol.

This time, I would hover very closely.

Chapter 10

If Bella's response to seeing her mum had been both emotional and regressive (her appetite was extremely poor for the next few days – in solidarity, perhaps?) her response to news of her stepfather was entirely different.

'He's been discharged from hospital,' Sophie told her, at the beginning of the following week. She'd come round specifically for the purpose of imparting this news.

Bella's reaction was immediate. 'He hasn't gone home to our house, has he?' she wanted to know. She looked anxiously at me. 'They wouldn't let him, would they? There's all the forensics! And what if *he's* seen where I'm living?' She was becoming increasingly agitated. 'He might be angry at me and come looking for me!'

So, finally, the reasons why Bella should avoid putting stuff on Facebook had sunk in. And she was right. Her father could have seen her whereabouts as easily as anyone else. Not that our joint foray onto the site had borne much other fruit; not in terms of actual intelligence. Well, other than the fact that Bella – not long twelve – had already amassed some three hundred-odd friends, including old friends and new friends and various mums of friends, too, because, she told me, 'Mums always like to be friends with you if you let them. It's so they can see what you're up to once you're a teenager.'

I had elicited Tyler's view on that point. 'Course they do,' he'd told me, looking surprised that I'd even asked about it. 'She's completely right. How else d'you think they're going to keep an eye on them. *D'oh*, Mum!'

He'd then gone on to point out that people used social media in different ways. Some used the 'don't put up anything you wouldn't want your granny seeing' system, which obviously meant much of interest to interested adults was filtered out. 'Anyway, we've got WhatsApp and Snapchat for important stuff now,' he added, winking mysteriously.

I didn't enquire further. There was a whole cyber-world I didn't yet know about, and I could barely keep up with what I *did* know about, even with the various social media seminars that were put on for foster carers. Anyway, what was of more interest to me currently was that Tyler had explained that Bella had probably got her privacy settings set to 'friends', and that unless she configured it differently, if she wrote on someone's timeline, or tagged them in a post, not only they but also *their* friends could see what was written, even if they weren't friends with Bella herself.

Which meant that, in theory, a *lot* of people could have found out where we lived, particularly if they had a vested interest in doing so.

I was unable to answer Bella's question, however, so had to look to Sophie, who was already shaking her head. 'No, he hasn't, sweetie,' Sophie said to her. 'Well, apart from to get stuff, of course. I believe he's rented a flat somewhere locally.'

Because the family home *was* still a crime scene, I wondered? Oh, how I wished we were allowed to know more of what was going on, however inappropriate – and therefore unlikely – I knew that to be. In another life, I would dearly love to be a detective. 'But why on earth would you think he'd be angry with you anyway?' Sophie asked Bella.

'Because,' Bella said, looking increasingly irritable now, too, 'I never went to visit him in hospital, did I?' She went on, in a tone that suggested it had been much on her mind since, 'I went to see Mum in prison, didn't I? But I never went to see him. He probably thinks I hate him, or something.'

'I'm sure your dad understands why you didn't,' I said, privately wondering if her reasons for not going had been as clear-cut as they'd seemed at the time. He'd been her stepdad for almost all her life, after all. Was there a part of her that still loved him? The sober him, at least? Certainly something to reflect on. 'But don't you worry, love. If you aren't ready to see him yet then you certainly won't have to.'

'Of course you won't,' Sophie reiterated. 'It's entirely up to you. Perhaps you'd rather write to him. You can do that instead, if you like. Perhaps you'd find that easier? Same as with your mum – put anything you like, and Casey will cast her eyes over it. I'm sure he'd be glad to hear from you, don't you think?'

To which Bella responded that she would. But then didn't. Over the next three days, she wrote twice to her mother and once to her friend Ruby, but the letter to her stepdad remained unwritten. And I found myself wondering even more about the court case that I knew was being prepared, which would impact so greatly on Bella's future, but about which we knew so little. And that comment she'd made – *my dad, but it's mostly been about my mum* – and how we knew so little, period. What exactly *had* been the events leading up to that day? Was there a real chance the contents of the note by the 'concerned citizen' were correct; that they held the greater truth?

What was becoming clearer by the day was that Bella wasn't going to be joining the local comp any time soon. And perhaps that was the correct way; suppose she started, began to settle in and then another upheaval happened? A court case could take months to prepare but it could equally, if reasonably cut-and-dried, take substantially less than that to come to trial. And at that point, Bella's world might implode yet again, and she could end up on a completely new trajectory – either back with her mother or in a new long-term foster placement or even, depending on the outcome, an adoptive home. So, much as I thought school would be the best place for Bella in the short term, given that she simply wasn't robust enough at the moment, I knew events might overtake my plans to see her there.

Which left the two of us spending a great deal of time together. An unhealthy amount of time, truth be known (and far too much housework-and-toddler-focused), so I decided I needed to find more constructive ways to occupy her.

Getting her out and about was a key goal. If there was a chance of integrating Bella into school I was anxious to grab it, and I knew it would happen much slower, if at all, if she remained indoors, hiding away from the world for too long.

For starters, I decided we needed to book a half-term holiday. We'd been toying with the idea anyway, as we liked taking Tyler away, but had sort of shelved the idea because of the wedding being imminent, both on a prohibitive-cost and a too-much-to-do basis.

'And you think I can now just go and book a week off?' Mike pointed out, when I ran my idea by him that evening, as a bolt-on to the details of Sophie's visit.

'Can't you jiggle things?' I asked him hopefully. 'Do some swaps? Offer to do some overtime, maybe?'

He looked at me with every bit as much disdain as I'd anticipated. Which was quite a lot, given he'd already booked off the week after Riley's wedding, so we could look after their three while they snatched a few days away for a honeymoon.

'I'll see what I can do,' he grumped. 'Though don't hold your breath.'

And, of course, I did hold my breath, albeit mentally rather than physically, though I reined myself in on planning where we'd go and what we'd do – well, bar making it clear to a disappointed Tyler that it wouldn't be skiing – on the 'prohibitive-cost-and-quadruple-it' basis.

And, in the meantime, anxious to get Bella out and about locally, I spent as much time as I could ferrying her to both Riley and Lauren's, the former as she loved helping make favours for the wedding, and the latter so she'd be comfortable enough with Lauren that she'd be happy to go to dance classes when they resumed.

I also took her down to my sister Donna's café, the latest 'in a line of unwitting Victorian child-labourers', as she usually put it, such was their enthusiasm for stacking the dishwasher, cleaning trays and wiping tables. This latter was a double plus, as Bella was soon happy to be left there to 'do a shift', giving me a much needed time-out to whizz into town for a breather, or run some errands for my mum and dad. Or, occasionally, just sit in a heap.

It was after returning from one such sortie a couple of weeks later that another idea struck me – one that, once I'd thought of it, I wondered why I hadn't thought of before.

Donna's café had a little bookcase library in the corner, of the increasingly popular 'donate and take away' variety, which meant she had a rolling stock of all sorts of reading material for the regulars to choose from.

I'd returned from dropping my mum home at that point when there tended to be a lull on a weekday – after the lunchers had mostly gone home, but before the mums-and-kids after-school rush hour.

Bella was down on the floor in front of the bookcase, surrounded by books, which she was presumably tidying and ordering before restocking. Except she wasn't. Out of sight of Donna, behind the till, she was cross-legged on the floor, apparently lost in some huge hardback tome.

I gestured to Donna, who leaned over the counter to see her.

'I'd have given money to see mine that interested in reading,' she whispered. 'Any chance she gets, she's got her nose in one of those books.' She leaned further over the counter. 'I just hope it's not something entirely inappropriate,' she added. 'You never know what's going to end up in there, not with some of our flipping regulars. I had to prune out *Fifty Shades* last week, so's not to offend the WI ladies. Though, between you and me, I suspect one of them might have sneaked it in. Ahem. Naming no names, of course ...'

Bella was in fact reading a Harry Potter book. Much thumbed, so probably old.

'Haven't you already read that one?' I asked her, squatting down to say hello.

'Oh, about six times,' she replied. 'But you never get tired of reading them again, do you?'

I thought her 'you' in this case was a bit of a royal 'we', at least where my personal HP habits were concerned. But my ignorance about the young wizard was obviously my problem, not hers. And that's when it hit me. The library. Why didn't I enrol her at the library? We had an all-singing-all-dancing library in town these days, courtesy of a sizeable chunk of lottery funding.

I was just about to suggest it, when she went on. 'I just love Harry Potter. One of my big dreams is to go to King's Cross one day ...'

'King's Cross?' I said, wondering why on earth anyone would want to go to such a historically grim part of

London. Then the penny dropped. 'Ah, you mean the *station*!' I said. 'That's where they go through a wall, isn't it?'

'Though the portal on platform nine and three-quarters,' she clarified.

'It actually *exists*, then?'

'Lord, Case, your ignorance is unbelievable!' Donna chipped in. 'Where have you *been* for the last twenty years?' She grinned at Bella. 'Ignore my peasant of a sister,' she added, laughing. 'She wouldn't know who Dumbledore was if her life depended on it.'

'And her life *might* depend on it, mightn't it?' Bella said, smiling back.

Which, of course, gave me another idea. Perhaps that was what we should do with our half term – or at least part of it. Go to King's Cross, so she and I could *both* see it for ourselves. Why not? If such a thing – place, portal, whatever – did exist, Tyler would be beside himself with excitement as well.

'Well,' I said, 'in that case, we'd better see if we can get ourselves there, hadn't we? And with half term coming up …'

Bella was on her feet in seconds. 'Oh my God, can we really? *Really*? And of course it exists, silly! There's a Harry Potter shop there too, and you can have photos taken on a broomstick, wearing the special scarf and everything. My friend went and she said it was magical. Oh my God. Can we really? I'm *so* excited!'

'Well, I'm not,' Mike said that evening when, tea done with, I told him all about having enrolled Bella at the big library and, having laid the ground, run my London plans by him as well. 'First up, it'll cost an arm and a leg, and secondly, it'll be hell on earth traipsing round London at half term. And thirdly,' he added before I could interrupt him with my pre-prepared flood of positivity, 'I don't think I'm going to be able to take the time off in any case.'

'What about one of the weekends?' I suggested, having already anticipated this obstacle.

He shook his head. 'Now that really *would* be lunacy. Less trains, more traffic, more people … Casey, that's an insane idea and you know it.'

I was just about to suggest that he lighten up and try to live a little when he put a hand up. 'But you could always take them yourself,' he said.

'What, on my own?'

'Why not?'

'Because it's London. Because it's miles away. Because I might lose one of them. Because it's –'

'Tyler's fifteen, love, not five. He'd be a help, not a hindrance. And that way I get to keep some annual leave days for the week in Spain we're going to need when the Wedding of the Century is over.'

'Oh, do stop calling it that,' I said. 'You know how much it winds Riley up.'

'It's meant to. But I'm serious. Wouldn't you rather that than me trailing along behind the Potter fan club, grousing and moaning?'

I would rather have a week in Spain on the horizon than pretty much anything, I decided. Whenever it turned out that we were able to take it. Which, given Bella's open-ended stay, might be a bit of a way away yet. But by then it would be summertime ... and hot ... and *away*.

'You know what?' I said. 'I am definitely warming to the idea.'

'And you could always take your mum to London with you,' he suggested.

I gave the idea at least half a second's thought. My mum, who thought a trip to the big department store in the adjacent city was a major expedition these days. Bless her, but no. She might even try and head right through into Diagonal Alley, or whatever it was called. I shook my head. 'Now her I *would* lose,' I said.

Chapter 11

Bella's excitement about the impending trip to London eclipsed just about everything over the coming days, including her anxiety about her stepdad. And as I'd now confirmed Tyler could bring Denver along too (so he wouldn't be 'completely swamped by girls') he was pretty excited as well.

As for me, I was just grateful that provided I booked trains at *very* specific times, and installed us in a small, basic hotel at some far-flung end of the Underground system, the trip would still leave me with an arm intact, even if not a leg. And, privately, though I was making much of the gruelling expeditionary nature of our adventure, this was strictly for Mike's ears. I was actually quite excited myself. Some youngsters have a pre-university gap-year to prepare themselves for the coming slog – I was having my own, pre-wedding stress gap-weekend.

Trust John Fulshaw to pour cold water on my happy planning.

It was early evening, and Bella and Tyler were watching an episode of *CSI: Crime Scene Investigation* together – Ty's favourite programme, and something they'd taken to doing quite a lot – when John called.

'I would have come to the house, Casey,' John said, 'but what I need to share with you can't be said if there's any danger of Bella overhearing.'

So this was something serious. Slipping my head round the living-room door to check both kids were engrossed, I braved the freezing cold weather and took the phone out to the back porch.

It was already dark, of course, and so cold that my wooden seat by the back door had already frosted over, so instead I paced up and down the back path, as he explained what he'd called about.

'I'm not sure how much of this is post Mr Cummings being discharged from hospital, and running around gathering support,' he said, 'or whether they already had a fair bit while he was still in ITU, but it would seem that the police now appear to have a substantial amount of evidence that supports a very different scenario to the one Bella's mum had them believe. Honest, Casey, you just never know, do you?'

He began quoting snippets at me – presumably gathered following interviews the police had conducted – and I listened in astonishment as he read out statements from neighbours, friends and even work colleagues, all of which suggested that the 'drunken attack' on Laura Daniels that had been the presumed order of events wasn't as clear cut and unprovoked as it seemed.

According to these potential witnesses, Laura Daniels was a world away from the down-trodden wife she had appeared to be. 'One here,' John said. I could hear bits of paper being shuffled. 'She says Laura "regularly taunted her partner by screaming that he wasn't a real man, and that she could get anyone she wanted at any time". Another one here – this is from a close neighbour – "a complete hussy. Always gets herself dolled up to go to work" – she worked at a town-centre bar, you'll remember – "leaving poor Adam at home looking after her kid".'

There was more. Another 'friend of the family' had claimed that Laura was very good at 'acting the innocent', but that, in reality, she goaded Adam into fights all the time, and that she was the one who drove him to drink, when all he wanted to do was to kick the habit.

'It just doesn't fit,' I said, trying to get my head around it. 'We certainly aren't short of candidates for the title of "concerned citizen" now, are we?'

'Coming out of the woodwork,' John agreed.

'But it's still weird,' I said. 'I mean, I know I haven't met either Laura or Adam Cummings, but the way that Bella and her mum are – the letters they write and the way Bella pines for her – this picture of her as some loud-mouthed neglectful floosie just doesn't fit.'

'I know how it seems, Casey,' John said. 'But don't forget, certain kinds of parents can be very manipulative when trying to impress social services or the police. Truth is that Laura Daniels could be everything she's described as *and* be devoted to her daughter. And don't forget, kids themselves tend to idealise their parents in these situations. She could be the mother from hell – doesn't mean Bella doesn't love her to bits.'

That I did know. 'But the same might apply to Adam Cummings, might it not? He might have that sort of personality – a born charmer. Remember Spencer's dad? He had *everybody* fooled.'

Spencer had been a boy we'd fostered a few years back who'd taken himself to social services, and the story was – and everyone had been taken in, and for a *long* time – that his poor parents didn't rush to have him back as they simply couldn't cope with him. That his poor dad, in particular, was at the end of his tether. At his wits' end, trying to know how to do his best for the boy, while taking care of his other siblings.

Turned out the father was a narcissist who had everyone duped. He'd seemed so plausible, when in reality, in the comfort of his own home, he'd been abusing poor Spencer since babyhood. Neglect. But also mind games, extreme mental cruelty. No, I wasn't going to take the word of neighbours at face value, even if it was all down in black and white on police notepaper.

'Good point,' John admitted. 'And, at the end of the day, it's not our business to be worrying about it. Our duty is simply to protect Bella and give her a safe place to stay while the whole sorry mess is sorted out. The question of who is right and who is wrong isn't ours to ponder. I'm just sharing this with you to prepare you that we might be in for a longer haul than we first thought. You okay with that?'

'John, you seriously need to ask that?'

'Just box ticking,' he said, allowing himself a little chuckle.

But it was a sobering reminder not to try and second guess the outcome of this. Because the truth was that the ultimate box that got ticked now for Bella was where she went next.

And possibly for the rest of her childhood.

It went without saying that none of this information should filter through to our young charge, and that for her life would go on as normal. For which the trip to London was an excellent distraction. I had also badgered Mike remorselessly about how I needed new clothes and shoes – after all, London was practically abroad, as far as I was concerned, so I both needed to look suitably togged up (as, of course, did Bella – the boys had a 'look' for all ports of call and all seasons), and have stout walking shoes to step out in, as well.

He finally agreed to the shoes.

So far so good, and the week before half term passed peacefully. No developments transpired, and I was glad that they hadn't. Due process of law would roll on without us, and perhaps the less we heard while it was doing so, the better.

The mood in the house was as a consequence buoyant – that fact endorsed when Bella had written to her mum, sounding as breathless with excitement as she was in person and, despite John's new intelligence, I couldn't help seeing her through Bella's eyes, and feeling happy that she'd be reassured that her little girl was okay.

But I was about to be thrown another curve ball. It was the Thursday before we were set to go on the Saturday, Tyler at school and Bella in town – since Lauren was making the trip with little Dee Dee, she had offered to take her with them.

With a couple of hours to myself, I'd just returned from the supermarket; I'd decided to stock up on bits and pieces to see Mike over the weekend, even though I knew full well he'd become a roving eating machine given half a chance, alternating between Kieron and Riley's.

It would be either that or he'd be home eating rubbish all weekend, while sitting watching sports on TV.

I had just stepped into the hall, shopping bags in hand, and kicked the door closed behind me when the doorbell began to ring. Placing my carrier bags down, and still wearing my coat and scarf, I re-opened the door to find a woman standing there, looking decidedly angry. She looked to be in her early thirties, slim, blonde and pink cheeked – obviously cold, despite a thick leather jacket and knee-length boots.

'So you're Casey Watson, then?' were the first words she spat at me.

'Sorry?' I asked, confused. 'Yes. Can I help you?'

The woman looked fit to burst a blood vessel. 'I'm here to give you a piece of advice, love,' she said, one hand on her hip. 'If you know what's good for you, you'll keep your nose out of our family business.'

'Look,' I said, clutching my scarf to my neck. 'I don't know who you are, and I have absolutely no idea what you're talking about. So can you please leave before I call the police?'

'Sounds like something you'd do!' The woman went on, 'I'm Adam Cummings's sister.' She pointed a finger at me

– French manicured, I noticed. 'And, like I said, you know nothing about anything! Keep your fucking nose out of our business,' she went on, before I could point out that she'd not, in fact, said that, 'and don't even think about slagging my brother off to the coppers, okay? And mark my words – if you don't fucking keep out of it, you'll be sorry, *very* sorry!'

So was this our 'concerned citizen'? I could feel adrenaline begin to pump. I was getting angry now. This bloody woman screaming on my doorstep – who the hell did she think she was?

'Look,' I said, raising my own voice now. 'You are clearly mixing me up with somebody else, but if you have supporting evidence for your brother, then it's the police you need to speak to – not me. I have nothing to do with any of that. Nothing at all. Now if you'd kindly leave, I'd be very grateful. I've heard what you have to say, and I don't want to hear any more of it.'

She stepped back then, off the doorstep, back to the path, where she stood and glared at me. 'Too right you've heard me,' she finished. 'And don't say you haven't been warned!' Then she turned around and stomped off back to the gate.

She didn't close it, but I stood and watched as it closed on her by itself, watching as she stalked off back down the road without a backwards glance. And as I went back inside, closing the front door, and also locking it, a thought occurred to me. If this woman *was* Adam's sister, then why on earth had she not once asked about Bella? How she was. If she was okay. Normal 'auntie' type stuff like that.

Adam Cummings's sister, my foot. Why hadn't I confronted her? I had to stop myself from running after her.

Chapter 12

I managed to get through to John Fulshaw on his personal mobile number. I only liked to use that in emergency situations: if it was something non-urgent that I needed to tell him out of hours, I generally preferred to leave a message on his work phone.

This wasn't out of hours, but I knew he wouldn't be in the office. He'd already told me earlier in the week that he was off at some conference or other, but I knew he wouldn't mind. This needed reporting now. I knew I would have to also report it to the police, as standard procedure, but I wanted to speak with him before I did that.

'Yes, of course, Casey, get straight on to the police,' John said after I'd explained what had happened. 'And I tell you what, it's probably a good thing you've planned to take Bella away for a few days, as I don't think her social worker would be too happy about this latest threat.'

'I agree,' I said. 'First thing that occurred to me. But the threat was directed at me and Mike, definitely not Bella. Though, I tell you what, the thing that's stuck most in my mind is that if she's her auntie she would surely want to know how Bella was, wouldn't she? Yet she didn't even bother to ask. Not once. Didn't even mention her.'

'Well, as there's no love lost between Bella and the other side of the family, I wouldn't count on that. And he's her stepdad – not her real father – so perhaps there's little contact. But I don't think she can be an aunt of Bella's because surely we'd all know about her. Yet there's no mention in any of the paperwork about Adam Cummings having a sister – and that would have been established early on because, had there been one, she might have been able to take her in. Absolute number one scenario social services and the police would have looked at, as you know. Specially when the maternal grandparents were ruled out. Very odd indeed. And not on, dammit. You okay?'

I assured him I was fine – only sorry that I'd not called her out, and after a brief conversation about what should happen next, John told me he would call an emergency strategy meeting for some time the following morning. I told him that I'd arrange for Riley to take Bella out for a couple of hours and that I'd be ready first thing. I then hung up and phoned the police, silently praying, as I reported what had happened, that they wouldn't take hours to get to me and take my statement. This was an iron that needed striking while it was hot.

I called Lauren then, and quickly explained what had happened, and she agreed to keep Bella till the police had left me and I could give her the all-clear. 'Leave her for as long as you need to,' she said. 'I'll tell her that you're still running around trying to get everyone sorted before you go away. She'll be fine.'

I only hoped I could convince John of that.

Thankfully, the police arrived not long after. One of them was the same officer who had spoken to me after I'd received the letter, and he nodded sagely as he deduced it was likely that it was the same person. 'I flipping hope so,' I said with feeling. 'Either that or he's got sisters sprouting everywhere!'

My statement made, I then – finally – unpacked all the shopping and, as Mike appeared before Tyler, who was – as per usual – out with Denver, I was able to fill him in too, before instructing him to drive to Kieron's and get Bella.

'Bloody hell!' he said, picking up the jacket he'd only just taken off. 'Quite a day then. You okay? Must have shaken you up a bit.'

I assured him I was fine – because I *was* fine. She'd been a scrap of a woman, really. And my principal emotion was one of irritation. How dare she! And who *was* she? Some girlfriend, I supposed. Some girlfriend who clearly had an axe to grind – but why? It wasn't as if Adam Cummings was in the dock, after all.

'I'll just be glad to get away, to be honest,' I told Mike, because I was. If only to stop my brain working overtime, thinking about things that I had no business thinking about. She was misguided on that front. I'd never met either of Bella's parents. Did she *really* think I'd have any influence in the coming court case?

Or that, ultimately, I'd even be so presumptuous. No, I was definitely glad to be getting away. It was her 'personal family business' and she was welcome to it. 'In fact if I had one of those broomsticks that Bella was raving about,' I told Mike, 'I might have already hopped on it and scooted off somewhere exotic. Did wizards scoot?'

Mike laughed. 'I have no idea. But I imagine so. Actually, love, speaking of exotic places, you remember my mate at work who has the caravan?'

I did, of course. We had rented it from him a few years back, to take away another couple of foster kids, in fact. 'Yes,' I said. 'Why?'

'Well, it's not in Wales any more. He's moved it to a place in Yorkshire, Primrose Valley I think it's called, and wouldn't you know, I was telling him about your madcap trip to London. And he said we were welcome to use it after – you know, for half term. So it's a shame I can't get away.'

'You're sure you can't?'

'You *know* I can't.'

'You're jealous, aren't you? Admit it. You want to come and see Platform 9.'

'Platform nine and three-quarters.'

'See, you really *do*. I rest my case.'

John called back first thing the following morning, as I'd known he would, with news of the emergency meeting he'd already promised would need to happen.

'At your place, if that's good for you,' he said. 'Today, if possible.'

We both knew there was no possible about it. Though I'd tried to put it out of my mind as much as possible, and

Bella was completely oblivious, a stone of gloom had lodged itself in my gut and wouldn't go away. The truth was that she might not even still be with us to go to London. They might even take her away today.

That we'd been tracked down by a member of a child's family was quite rightly a red flag, since that child's safety was always going to be paramount. Not to mention ours. And given the backgrounds of some of the children we'd looked after down the years that wasn't something I was ever going to take lightly. So protocol dictated that the overwhelmingly obvious course of action would be to move Bella to another family as a matter of urgency.

I thought of her upstairs, humming to herself – actually *humming* – while she made a list of all the things she was going to take on holiday. 'Yes, that's fine, John,' I told him, keeping my voice low. 'But, you know, we can just as easily have this meeting once we're back from our weekend away, can't we? At least let her have that, surely? She's been so looking forward to it.'

Even as I spoke, I knew what John's response had to be. Much as he sympathised, and I knew he did, there were some things that were set in stone, and this was one of them.

'You know it's got to be today, Casey,' he said. 'Much as I wish it could be otherwise. But, you know, it's not absolutely a foregone conclusion that she'll need to leave you.'

'And a pig just flew past the window,' I said miserably. And a plague on the ever-extending tentacles of Facebook, I thought, but didn't say.

'I know,' John soothed. 'Look, I've just spoken to Sophie, and her line manager, Kathy Heseltine, and they are both okay for later on this morning. And they can bring along another social worker to take Bella out for lunch or something while we have the meeting. Thought it would be easiest that way. That okay?'

No, it wasn't okay, grateful as I was for their collective foresight. Being dragged off to some café or park somewhere by a complete stranger was the last thing Bella needed right now. It would only terrify her, wondering about what was going to happen to her next. 'I've already arranged it with Riley,' I said, because I had been just about to when he'd called and I knew she'd say yes. 'And she's happy for me to drop Bella round to hers for a couple of hours. Grateful even. Give her a chance to catch up with all the housework she's falling behind on while she's got her nose stuck in *Brides* magazine. And Bella loves entertaining Marley Mae. What sort of time are you thinking?'

'Around eleven,' John said. 'Or fairly soon after. Would that work for you?'

Not having the meeting at all was what would most work for me, I thought – but, again, didn't say. None of this was John's fault. Wasn't anyone's fault, truth be known, because I certainly wasn't blaming Bella. If she'd inadvertently led this woman to us, and that seemed a strong possibility, she'd certainly not done it intentionally. No, it was just another unexpected spanner in the already overstretched works. And we still didn't even know who the woman really was.

'That works fine,' I told him.

But it didn't feel fine. I was already expecting the worst.

As I expected, Riley was only too glad to take Bella off my hands for a couple of hours. 'I'm happy to keep her till school time, if you like,' she said. 'Hell, till tonight, if it suits you, Mum. I'm not sure which is climbing highest up the walls – me or the flipping ironing pile!'

And, equally as expected, Bella was only too happy to be dropped round to play with Marley Mae. 'I'll take my jewellery-making kit,' she decided, delving into her chest of drawers to pull it out. 'She loves helping me with that. And she's getting good at it too. She's making a secret bracelet for Riley, for a wedding present. Though we'd better not make that while we're at hers, had we?'

It was all said with such happy assurance that it frustrated me anew. Bella had been with us not quite two months, yet she spoke with such confidence about her new little friend's likes and dislikes. She was one of those children who you just knew would have made a natural older sibling. Little did she know the purpose of me taking her to the happy bustle of Riley's was so that her being taken away from us permanently – and, the way things usually worked, at a moment's notice, literally – could be discussed while she was safely out of the way.

And much as I wished it otherwise, I knew it was pretty much a done deal. Which did nothing for my mood as, with Bella duly dropped off at Riley's, smiling and blissfully ignorant that her fate was to be decided in her absence, I went back home and performed the usual pre-meeting rituals. Clearing the clutter, clearing the dining table, wielding the duster, polish and air freshener, amassing cups and saucers, rootling around in the cupboard for my trusty milk jug, laying out the usual selection of biscuits.

It wasn't going to be a large meeting. It didn't need to be. Just me, John, Sophie and her line manager, Kathy, who turned out to be a nice-seeming woman in perhaps her mid-fifties. She was really well spoken, and expensively dressed – something that a few years ago would have had me feeling inferior and out of place. These days, however, despite much of my work involving kids from the 'wrong' side of the tracks, it had put me in rooms and in meetings with people from *all* walks of life, and I had learned that no matter how one dressed or spoke, basically we were all the same.

We were all on the same team with regard to Bella, too, I reminded myself. So I really needed to stop feeling so adversarial. And, after the usual introductions, we soon got to the matter in hand – the crux of which was that Kathy, understandably, was extremely worried that an unknown (as yet) person had actually been to our house, and she was obviously concerned for Bella's safety.

'It's not unheard of for family members to snatch a child from their carers,' Kathy reminded us all. 'And, yes, I *know* it's unlikely, but our priority is Bella and we have to protect her as well as we can. Which is why I've been making enquiries into an alternative placement this morning.'

I could feel my face drop and I looked to John for help.

He smiled reassuringly. 'Casey, Kathy's been to Bella's previous carers this morning – first port of call, obviously

– to see if they were in a position to help out. Just for a few days, that's all. Just until the police can get to the bottom of who that woman was.'

This was encouraging news. So, if they could identify the woman, and if they didn't think she posed a major threat, perhaps, even if Bella was taken from us temporarily, we'd be able to have her back with us very soon. Though that still left the business of the trip to London. I was just about to say so, when John raised a hand, indicating that Kathy was going to explain further.

'Unfortunately,' she went on, 'they can't do anything just now, as they're busy helping look after their new grandchild. And I know you're off for the weekend, which is great, of course, but we still have to ensure that Bella is in a place of safety when you return.'

I decided a white lie would be a risk worth taking here. 'Actually, things have moved on since I spoke to you earlier, John. We can take Bella away for the whole of half-term week. We have the keys to a caravan in Yorkshire, you see – Mike's work colleague – and we've planned to go straight on up there after London. Does that make a difference?'

It would definitely make for an interesting phone conversation with my husband once they'd gone. But one way or another, I knew we could do this, even if I had to play the 'greater good' and 'Mike's fostering responsibilities' cards with his boss myself. Anyway, he was the manager, wasn't he? Surely he could twiddle with the rota?

The three others in the room glanced at one another, and, seemingly unable to come up with an objection to that, Kathy nodded. 'Well, that would certainly solve our problem in the short term ...' she mused.

'Wouldn't it?' I said brightly, conscious that John was looking at me through narrowed eyes. 'Perfect timing, eh? God bless that man with a van, eh?'

'Right, then,' John said. 'Well, I suppose any more drastic plans could wait until the Watsons get back from their Yorkshire trip, can't they? And it'll give us a bit of space to see if we can find out who this woman might be.'

Kathy nodded. 'It'll certainly give us a bit of breathing space,' she said, then, looking pointedly at me, 'but you do understand, Casey, don't you, that if we haven't resolved the matter of the so-called sister turning up at your house by the time you get back, we'll have to revisit our plans to move Bella?'

'Of course I do,' I assured her, 'and thank you for letting us take her away, too. I really appreciate it. Bella's finally in a place where she feels comfortable around us – the extended family too, particularly my little granddaughters. We've come such a long way, and I'd hate to disrupt all that now.'

'I know,' Kathy said. 'And I absolutely sympathise. But if that's what has to happen, then I'm afraid it still will.' She sighed deeply, and daintily picked up a biscuit. The only one of the meeting thus far. I was put in mind of the Queen and the thing I'd once heard about no one being able to start eating at a dinner until she'd picked up her cutlery. Nothing queenly about Kathy, though. I suspected she had to make some pretty down-and-dirty decisions in her job.

'I know,' I said. 'Flipping Facebook.'

'I think I'd use a stronger word. I know I sound like a dinosaur but I so *abhor* the problems all these social media channels have given us. Oh the trials of the digital age, eh?'

Kathy broke the biscuit in two and popped half in her mouth. Respect to her. I reckoned she knew a bit more about social media than me too.

The remainder of the meeting went as smoothly as could be expected. We had a general update and chat about how things currently were, and how they were looking longer term, and I agreed that, after Kathy and John left, Sophie would stay behind with me so that she could ask Bella if she could shed any light on who our caller might have been.

'No skirting round the houses,' Kathy said. 'We need her to be asked outright about this so-called aunt of hers. Hopefully Adam Cummings himself will be able to clarify the position re the complement of so far unaccounted-for relatives he might have, but he's currently not answering calls – either to us or the police. Which probably means nothing – he could be out and about, with his lawyer, anything really. But from what you've reported, she sounds spurious. I think we're all agreed on that point, aren't we?' We all nodded. 'And who knows,' Kathy finished, 'Bella herself might be able to shed light on who she actually might be. Anyway, we'll leave you in peace.'

'And, you know what, Casey,' Sophie said, 'I could go and grab some lunch in town, if you like. You know – give you a chance to get straight, go and pick Bella up – come back in a couple of hours? Would that suit you?'

I agreed it made sense. No point in Sophie hanging around while I drove over to Riley's to pick Bella up. I waved them off, telephoned Riley, and set off to fetch Bella, glad that at last we'd been given the go-ahead to ask her. Since I felt almost certain the woman had tracked us down via Bella speaking to her friend on Facebook, I felt sure she'd be able to shed some light on things. I only hoped it didn't plunge us into further darkness.

It didn't really get us anywhere, in the end. I sat in on things, and could tell straight away that Bella was as clueless as we were.

'He doesn't have a sister,' she told Sophie, immediately she had put the question to her. 'Or a brother. Or anyone, as far as I know. Not that I've ever heard talked about or met,' she added.

Sophie explained about the woman turning up and professing to be her stepdad's sister, and as she did so I could see the anxiety growing in Bella. Sophie had me describe her. Again, Bella shook her head. 'It's definitely not a sister,' she said again. 'I know that for sure. He said it lots to me – that we were both only children. So who was that woman, then? What did she want?'

Here I knew Sophie would be necessarily sparing with the details. 'We're not sure,' she said. 'She wasn't looking for you or anything like that,' she said, glancing at me. 'I think, in her funny way, she just wanted Casey here to know that your stepdad was, um, okay – doing well, you know? And that, well ...' She shrugged. 'Just that she was his friend.'

Now Bella looked animated more than scared. 'Well, he *definitely* doesn't have any of those.'

Chapter 13

Amazing how the prospect of adventure can take your mind off everything else, particularly when it's an adventure tinged with an element of anxiety, as any trip to the capital would be for a homebody such as me. It had also been many years since I'd last ventured to London, and I was sure it would have changed a great deal.

So, far from fretting about our angry visitor, the meeting, or the possible outcome of the meeting (which wobbly bridge I would cross if and when we came to it) I was almost as excited as the kids were as Mike dropped us off at the train station at stupid o'clock on Saturday morning. The kids were all puffy-eyed from lack of sleep, which – I know it's mad – gave me enormous pleasure. In our mile-a-minute world, with so many distractions available to children round every corner, it was good to see teenagers – and one almost-teenager, in Bella – so excited about the prospect of something as ordinary as a trip on a train, to see a train platform, in the company of a diminutive and slightly naggy middle-aged woman.

Though they'd be horrified to think it, Tyler and Denver were actually giggling together as Mike waved us off through the ticket barrier, and Bella, who'd not said a further word about recent developments, couldn't seem to stop grinning.

'Now remember your promise, kids,' I said, for what was already probably the fourth time. 'We all stick together, look out for each other, and never let anyone out of our sight. London is a massive place. *Massive*. And we could easily get lost in it.'

Denver patted my arm. 'Stop panicking, Mrs W. I've been to the smoke twice, so I know my way round it. Don't worry. I won't let any of you get lost.'

Mike stuck a thumb up. 'I'm counting on that, kiddo,' he said. And while I wasn't – for all his 'smoke' stuff, Denver couldn't possibly know his way round more than a tiny fraction of it – I was definitely reassured by having two strapping fifteen-year-olds with me: safety in numbers. I just wished I could act on my small-hours idea, to have us all roped together, like mountaineers.

Still, the excitement was the main thing, and once we were safely boarded I felt relaxed enough to lose myself in the moment a little more. Though it seemed Bella still had other things on her mind. We'd not been able to bag a table so were sitting in two rows of two, the boys in front of us, and we'd not long left the suburbs behind when she tapped me lightly on the forearm with Dobby, who'd she brought along for the ride. (Something of an added worry in itself; I'd seriously wondered if I could get a tracker fitted for him.)

'Casey, you know that woman?' she whispered, cupping her hand around her hand and leaning close to my left ear.

I leaned in too. 'Yes,' I whispered back, as conscious as she was that we'd not discussed any of this with Ty yet.

'Well, I was thinking last night about who she might be, and I wondered if she might be from the club he used to go to.'

'He' as in her stepdad. 'What sort of club?' I asked.

'I'm not sure,' Bella said. 'But he used to go there lots. And my mum used to get cross.' She fell silent.

'What, like a sports club?' I suggested.

She shook her head. 'Well, I don't think so. He didn't wear different clothes or anything.'

'I see,' I said, not sure whether to quiz her further. 'Well,' I eventually replied, having opted just to file it for now. 'That's all very helpful, sweetie. I'll bet that's it. Maybe she was just wondering where he'd got to, eh?'

Then something else obviously occurred to Bella. 'That's why I thought of it,' she whispered. 'My stepdad's on Facebook.'

Luddite I may be but in this I was already one step ahead of her. Not any more he wasn't, sadly.

'Is that it?' I announced, some three and a half hours later.

Excitement was at fever pitch by the time we had finally arrived at King's Cross. And remained up there, despite the alarming numbers of people, the enormous queues and the real possibility that I might lose all three charges at any moment. And for this? This brick wall with a trolley embedded in it?

But I was clearly in a minority of one. Just like every other person who was milling about, amid the sea of clicking smartphones, Ty, Denver and Bella were completely rapt.

'I can't believe we're actually here,' Bella breathed, clutching Dobby tightly to her chest, as if he was a badge of office, or a magic talisman.

'Nor can I,' I agreed, though for rather different reasons. We were now in the epicentre of noisy, smelly London – for this! 'Don't we get to go through anything?' I wanted to know. 'Isn't that the whole point of it?'

And was rewarded for my ignorance with a short lecture from all three of them about how only wizards could do that – didn't I know *anything*? – and how this was more than enough – this was all about just *being* here. Apparently.

And having your photo taken for posterity, obviously. 'By the wall, Mum,' Tyler explained. 'And you have to wear a Harry Potter scarf and hold a broomstick and do a funny jump.'

Obviously.

'There's a great shop, though,' Denver added. 'You'll *definitely* like the shop, Mrs W.'

So that was me told. And he certainly had my number about the shopping. But he was definitely wrong on this particular occasion. *Great*, I thought. So we get to queue here for God knows how long, just to see a wall with half an old trolley stuck in it, and my highlight is that I then get to shuffle round an overcrowded shop, and spend lots of money on things I neither know or care about. I was beginning to understand how Mike felt when he came shopping with me …

But I wasn't Mrs Grumpy for long. When we finally reached our accommodation (via the Tube, which was another scary nightmare) and the beds were variously allocated and bounced on, a bout of further online research revealed that the bit of the trip I *hadn't* told them about – a visit to the actual Harry Potter Studio Tour tomorrow – would be a journey of only slightly nightmare-ish proportions in comparison to the one we'd just made. Yes, it was more of an extravagance than we could strictly afford, but I knew it would be worth every single hard-earned penny just to see the expressions on their faces.

And I wasn't wrong. I told them over pizza in a nearby Italian restaurant chain, and their combined response when I told them what our plans were for Sunday was sufficient to have diners at nearby tables drop cutlery, splurt drinks and leave their seats.

'Best. Day. *Ever*,' was Tyler's considered response on calming down and finally releasing me from a bear hug. No amount of money could buy that.

Thankfully, the studio tour was definitely of a 'that's a bit more like it' kind of place. Another lengthy journey, yes, and an acquaintance with another couple of vast, busy stations, but once we were there it was as if we really had stepped into a film set. Well, film set after film set, because that's what we were doing; from the Great Hall, to Diagon Alley – with the famous Ollivanders wand shop (a great draw for Denver) to Gringotts Bank, to Dumbledore's office with all its treasures, and as we shuffled round (again, there was much shuffling to be done there) I realised I'd absorbed a lot more of the world of wizards than I'd known – perhaps by some wizardly osmosis.

Best of all, however, was a call I got while they were busy sipping 'butterbeer' (which was, to my mind, beyond revolting).

It was Mike.

'Lost any of them yet?' were his first words.

'Certainly not!' I huffed at him. Though this was obviously a lot more by luck than judgement. 'Anyway,' I said, once I'd regaled him with an update on the morning's adventures, 'how is your day going, home all on your lonesome? You wish you'd come now, don't you? Admit it.'

'I'm not at home,' he said. 'I'm in the warehouse, hard at work.'

I was about to ask him why, but, of course, I knew straight away. 'So does that mean …?'

'Just about,' he said. 'Though I've had to jump through a *lot* of hoops. I'm here all day, and I'll have to pop in for a bit tomorrow morning, but that'll give you time to pack for the caravan, won't it?'

I'd half expected it, of course, because I knew that, despite what he'd said, Mike would do his very best – he wouldn't even have mentioned it otherwise. But it was still news I'd been crossing my fingers for. I assumed he'd pulled some strings, promised goodness knew what in terms of future overtime, or he'd perhaps even explained to the big boss that it was a fostering crisis he needed to be there for. But

I wasn't going to look a gift horse in the mouth by wanting chapter and verse on it – it was simply another opportunity to make three children (and, by extension, me) very happy, and that was good enough for me.

And as Mike had suggested, I did a lightning-quick Monday morning washing, drying and shopping turnaround, so that by mid-afternoon, the car loaded with children, supplies and lots of cold-weather gear, we were off on our way to what the weather forecast was already promising would be a chilly and perhaps even snowy Yorkshire. They talk about time zones – but we were crossing weather zones as well; even in the car we could see winter coming down to claim us; the hint of spring down in London already felt an impossible dream.

'Anyway, we're not going for the weather,' Tyler said, as I ran through the weather stats on my smartphone. 'I reckon it'll be more exciting if the weather's really, *really* bad and we have to struggle to survive.'

'You've been watching too many Bear Grylls shows on telly,' Mike observed, grinning. 'And I doubt there will be any likelihood of us struggling to survive. More likely struggling to get through the lorry load of food your mum's packed. Not to mention,' he added darkly, as we wheezed up a steepish hill, 'struggling to even get there, given the weight in this flipping car.'

Oh, my, though, when we got there it was cold beyond cold, as all logic should have already told us it would be. After all, what else was a caravan if not a tin box? So whoever went to stay in one in February? Not to mention one in Yorkshire …

'Lunatics, that's who,' Mike muttered as he returned from braving the elements – not to mention increasing flurries of the promised snow – in order to connect the gas bottle and put the water on. And it was touch and go whether we shouldn't just pack up again and drive home, because it was cold enough to freeze the water in the pipes, too – it was only a phone call to Mike's colleague, who assured us our body heat, plus the heater, plus the boiler and the insulation, and so on and so forth, meant we really didn't need to fret.

I wasn't so sure. Even with the fire on, you could tell from its meagre output that it would be a long time before it made any sort of impression on the Arctic chill.

Still, the kids, to a man (and a girl), thought it was brilliant.

'Going to a caravan in the summer is for softies,' Denver said decisively, once we were all installed in the little living room, huddled round the gas fire, each of us sitting in our sleeping bags.

That had been a good idea on Tyler's part. We'd put the little oven on as well, so we could warm up the chilli I'd brought for supper (cold, cold night, hot, hot food) and with my hands wrapped round a mug of coffee I was beginning to feel quite toasty.

The caravan responded with what sounded like its agreement – rattling, almost vibrating even, as it shuddered under the onslaught of a particularly fierce gust of wind. Perhaps we were lunatics, I thought. We certainly seemed to be the only people currently on site if the blackness beyond the caravan curtains was anything to go by.

'It sounds a bit like a helicopter landing on us, doesn't it?' Mike observed. 'You know, the way it rumbles when the wind gives it a battering.'

'I flipping hope not,' I said with feeling. 'Well, unless it was coming to pick us up and relocate us to one of the Costas,' I added.

'Oh, shurrup, Mum – you're loving this,' Tyler said, nudging me with his sleeping-bag-clad feet. And, of course, he was right. Despite all the obvious pointers that I shouldn't be – the snow, the cold, the blizzard – I really was.

'Perhaps it's Bear Grylls coming,' Denver said. 'Perhaps he's being winched down so he can do one of those survival programmes here, where he's got an hour to build a shelter and make a fire out of moss and twigs before all his toes drop off.'

'I can't quite imagine *that* would happen,' Mike said, chuckling. 'Not in an hour. Not in Yorkshire. Not if he's got his boots on, at any rate. And he really doesn't strike me as the kind of man who'd forget his boots.'

'Yeah, but it can still happen, Dad,' Tyler was quick to point out. 'If the altitude's high enough. Mountaineers lose fingers and toes all the time. And that's even with their gloves and boots *on*.'

'Well, happily, we're not up Everest,' I chipped in, before finishing my coffee. 'And we also have a heater, and lots of food.'

'*Lots* of food,' Mike agreed.

'And no one's going to be out in the elements tonight, booted or otherwise,' he added. He looked in my direction. Like me, the thought that Tyler and Denver might just want to had probably crossed his mind.

'But I wonder what it's like,' Denver said, confirming Mike was probably right. 'You know, if the caravan blew away or something and we all had to camp out. I wonder how quickly we'd die.'

'Denver! Enough of that,' I said. 'No one's dying of exposure on my watch, I can assure you.' I pulled the zip down and began wiggling out of my sleeping bag, to find the caravan air a welcome few degrees above freezing now, certainly sufficient for me to brave it and start on tea.

'Yeah, but I wonder what it would be like, being out in this. I reckon it might be fun,' Tyler said. 'You remember that school canoeing trip thing we did for PE, Denv? That was in, what, April? And we sat outside half the night with Mr Curtis to look at the stars?'

'*Did* you?' I said. 'You didn't mention that bit.'

'Mr Curtis told us not to,' Denver answered. 'In case our mums started fretting about us being out without our liberty bodices on. Whatever they are when they're at home. But, yeah,' he added, having drained his mug of tea, 'I reckon it would be well fun.'

'It won't.' We all turned. It was the first time Bella had spoken in a while. She'd been content to be snuggled down beside me on the back part of the sofa that ran round the end of the caravan, just listening, and sometimes laughing, while the boys rattled on.

'Really? How would you know?' Denver wanted to know. There was no edge in his tone, but even so I could feel Bella bristle slightly beside me.

'Because I've slept out,' she said simply. 'In the winter. Hallowe'en, it was. Last year. And I didn't have a caravan either. I didn't even have a tent.'

'You *never*,' Tyler said, sitting forward now, clearly impressed. 'What was this for? Was it in the Guides or something?'

Bella shook her head. 'Just at home. In my garden.'

'What, for a Hallowe'en dare or something?' Denver asked, also much impressed.

Again Bella shook her head, and I couldn't tell if she was revelling in the kudos or just keen to put her sixpence-worth in. In any event, she said, 'No, just because my parents were fighting.'

'So you stayed out all night, like?' Denver asked her. A not unreasonable question. 'Without a tent or anything? You must have been *frozen*.'

Tyler glanced at me before adding his own sixpence worth. 'But what about your mum and dad? Didn't they even notice? Where *were* they?'

'I didn't know and I didn't care,' Bella said. 'I just crawled under my old sandpit and slept underneath it.'

Both boys were now agog and I sensed we should probably call a halt to this. 'Well, that's you two put in your place,' I said, squeezing Bella's forearm as I stood up. 'And let's be clear – there'll be no camping out of any description tonight. Quite apart from anything else' – I pointed – 'there's a cliff just over there. Right. Time we got on, I think. Bella, d'you want to help me with the food? While Ty and Denver help Mike sort the table out and everything?'

Bella wriggled her way out of her own sleeping bag and followed me, and as she passed the boys Ty stuck a hand up to high-five her.

'Reee-spect, mate!' he said.

'I did, you know,' Bella whispered to me a couple of hours later as I tucked her and her faithful Dobby into bed. We'd given her the little bunk room to herself, while Ty and Denver shared the double sofa-bed in the living room. The snow hadn't abated but at least the wind had dropped now. The quiet outside was absolute. Goodness only knew what we'd wake up to in the morning.

I sat down on the edge of the bottom bunk, taking care not to crack my skull on the top one. 'I don't doubt that for a moment,' I said. 'Must have been scary, though.'

'Actually, it wasn't,' she said. 'I mean, it sort of was, but I think I was too upset to be scared. And then, when I realised they'd locked me out –'

'Locked you *out*? What, your mum and dad did?'

'Not my *mum*,' she corrected quickly. 'She'd *never* do that. Not on purpose. I mean, she did – but she didn't realise. She thought I was in bed.'

'How would she think that, love?'

'Because my stepdad was drunk and they were fighting. Just like they always do. And I *had* gone to bed, but then I came down to try and stop them because they were in the kitchen, which is underneath my bedroom, and it's just unbearable having to listen to them, trying to sleep. And my stepdad was, like, screaming at me to get out of his sight, like he always does, and – I don't know. I went into the living room and then I ran out into the garden. Just to get away from them, you know? From *him*. Just to get away from the *shouting*.'

'But how did you end up spending the night out there?'

She frowned. 'It wasn't quite the *whole* night – my mum came and found me … I don't know. At four o'clock or something. I'm not sure.'

'So *almost* the whole night, then,' I said, increasingly appalled by what I was hearing. 'But how, love?'

'Because my stepdad locked the patio door,' she said. 'My mum was telling him to shut up – the neighbours are, like, on at them all the time. They all hate us. Mr Atkinson – he's on one side of us – even got the police round one time. So my stepdad went across – I watched him – and banged the door shut and put the catch down.'

'But what about you? You know, when you saw that. Didn't you rush over there and try and stop him?'

Even in the dark bedroom, I could see Bella was looking at me as if I had a screw loose. 'You don't know my step-dad,' she said. 'Even when he seems okay, if you set him off, he's like a …' She paused, trying to find the word. 'Like he's just been waiting, you know? For a reason to start up again. And, it's like, I see my mum …' She looked up and the light spilling in from the little corridor glinted in her eyes. 'She just doesn't *get* that. You know, when he's been drinking and he's like that. Like you only have to *speak* to him and it's like, he's off on one again.' Another pause. 'She just never *gets* that.'

I touched my hand to her cheek, conscious of the bitter cold outside. It was warm. 'So you stayed put.'

A small nod. 'I was just still so *cross*. I didn't *want* to go back in there. I wasn't that cold. I had my dressing gown on …'

'But you didn't go back and even knock on the window? I mean, even later?'

She shook her head. 'I didn't want to. And by the time I did want to they had already turned the light off and stopped yelling. My mum had gone to bed.'

'She wouldn't have checked on you?' I asked mildly. (*She didn't even check on her*? I thought, rather less mildly.)

Again, Bella shook her head. 'She already had. And she wouldn't have wanted to wake me. She knows I'd have only been all upset. And my stepdad had probably passed out. Or gone out. It's usually one or the other. No, passed out. He was in his chair when we came back in again.'

'Oh, sweetheart. You must have been *terrified*.'

She shook her head. 'I really wasn't. I wasn't making that up. I mean, I got a bit cold … but I must have fallen asleep anyway, because I woke up to find my mum shaking me awake.'

'God, she must have had forty fits when she realised you weren't in bed!'

'She just cried a lot. Casey, that's all she does. Cry and cry. She just cries all the time.'

I put both arms around her and held her tight, not having the first clue what to say to her. And enough time passed that, before I'd so much as come up with anything, she spoke herself.

'I can't *bear it* when my mum cries,' she said.

Chapter 14

'You know what this has been?' Mike said as he hefted our holdalls from the boot of the car four short days later. 'It's been a stay of execution. That's all.'

It was now Friday, and a world away from our little holiday snow-dome bubble, which had been punctured by John Fulshaw before we were even half way home.

I took my bag from Mike, glancing past the car to check that the children were all in the house now, out of earshot. 'Mike, I *know* that. Doesn't mean I'm going to take it lying down, though.'

I did know, as well, because John had obviously been at pains to get hold of me. Full of apologies (we'd been in the car, of course, when he'd finally got through to me, so we hadn't been able to speak properly), but nevertheless keen to establish that we'd be meeting again, him, Sophie and Kathy, as was already half-arranged, first thing on the Monday morning.

Which I'd had no choice but to agree to, and without any discussion, since Bella, Ty and Denver were all right there in the back seat. (Dozing, yes, but dozing children still have ears.) But it didn't mean I hadn't already been scheming, pulling together my points to support what I knew to be true; that one thing trumped all the other arguments they'd put to me for moving her: that, as long as we could keep her safe, Bella's best interests would be so much better served if she stayed right where she was. Since her revelation that first evening (which wasn't so much a revelation as confirmation of everything I already suspected) she was opening up to me now, no question. Her last word that night had been that she was never, ever going to drink beer when she was a grown-up, because it made people into monsters, and since then she was making more and more references to her home life. She'd even alluded to the reason why she hated her granddad. 'He's a horrible old drunk man as well,' she had told me. 'My mum *hates* him. She says I must never, ever marry anyone who drinks lots.'

So the picture was developing, from a pencil sketch to the beginnings of the whole now. And it was surely only a matter of time before she finally let it go, and disclosed at least some of what had happened that particular night. Because no matter how badly she wanted to protect her mother, she was intelligent enough to know that she couldn't keep running from the truth, and that the evidence they already had might be enough alone for a jury to convict her.

There was also the point (and I knew it wasn't one it would be appropriate for me to raise with her) that even if her mum *had* hit her dad on the back of the head (which was a stark medical fact, not a matter of opinion), what

Bella had to say about the events that had preceded it could actually help her. While it was understandable that Bella didn't want to confirm that she'd seen the actual blow, she and she alone knew what had gone on between her parents that afternoon, and all the hearsay from neighbours and concerned citizens – not to mention spurious sisters – couldn't change that.

And there was clearly a pattern of violence – at least of regular violent arguments, at any rate – and if Bella could share examples such as she'd shared with me that evening it could all help her mother's case so much. She was due another visit from Katie, her counsellor, soon, too, and I could only hope that this time *she* would broach that conversation. I made a mental note that, as well as Bella's new disclosures, I must also share my thoughts on all that with John.

Well, if I was to be involved further, that was.

'Love, you can't fight this,' Mike said. 'Not if that's what they've already decided. You know that.'

'I know no such thing,' I huffed at him. 'It's not like we're dealing with an axe-murderer, after all. Just some silly, hysterical woman; honest, Mike, if you'd seen her you'd say the same, I know you would. I could have taken her down in no time.'

Mike burst out into a loud guffaw. 'Hark at you!' he said. 'Who are you? Vi Kray, or something? Or has all the Harry Potter stuff gone to your head and you think you can wave a wand and just go poof! Is that it?'

'No, of *course* not. Anyway, we need to get the bags in and get organised so you can drop Denver home while I put Bella to bed. I promised his mum we'd have him home to her before ten.'

'Yes, sir,' said Mike, with a slight edge to his voice. 'And meanwhile you have to promise me you're going to calm down, Case. And that you're not going to make any rash phone calls while I'm gone.'

'It's bloody nine o'clock on a Sunday night,' I huffed. 'Who exactly would I ring?'

I reached back into the footwell for my handbag and mobile, seething quietly, out of sight, while Mike headed in to round up Denver.

John hadn't exactly said it outright, but I could tell from the things he had said that, in the local authority's opinion, at any rate, Bella should definitely be moved on without delay. I hefted my bag up onto my shoulder and followed Mike inside. Well, not while I had any kind of say in it, she wouldn't.

I knew I wouldn't get much sleep that night, and I was right. Mike did, at least – he had to be up for work at six, so it was good to hear him snoring, but since I was wide awake (even the marathon country walk we'd done the previous afternoon hadn't helped) I was already up, dressed and had written a long email to John in the kitchen by the time he had showered and come downstairs.

'You okay, love?' he asked, pouring us coffees from the jug I'd made – his first, my third. 'I could always try to get Jim to cover for me later on, if you think I should. Nip home for an hour? If you really want me to, I will.'

I shook my head. 'No, it's fine,' I said. 'I'm calm now. And I promise I'm going to *stay* calm as well. I'll listen to what they have to say and then I'll say *my* piece. That's all I can do, isn't it?'

'It is, love,' Mike agreed as he sat down beside me. 'What about Bella, though? What are you going to say to her? What are you going to *do* with her? She must wonder why she keeps getting shipped out all the time.'

'Sorted,' I said, because I'd already made a plan. 'I've texted Lauren –'

'At this hour?'

'At this hour. Don't worry. She's already up as well. She's going to pick Bella up after Tyler's gone to school. They're going to the hall to do the paperwork.'

Mike looked confused. 'What hall? What paperwork?'

'The insurance documentation for the dance club,' I explained. 'She's taking Dee Dee with her so she needs Bella to mind her while she does it. So, yes, it's all sorted. Don't worry. She'll be excited to be involved.'

And she was, too. She skipped off with Lauren and Dee Dee happy as a sandboy, and a well-rested one, too, full of all the adventures we'd had the previous week. Which left me alone with a mound of washing and a meeting to host, and as I waved them off I tried to imagine how she'd react if she returned home, all smiles, to be told she'd be leaving us right away.

Which got my goat. She'd spent the whole week making such healing, happy memories, and if they took her now they would for ever be associated with the trauma and distress of being shipped off to strangers. I couldn't let that happen. Well, in truth, I couldn't stop it happening either.

But it made me all the more committed than ever to fighting to keep her with us.

I tried not to think of the three (or was it four?) horsemen of the apocalypse as the same unsmiling trio trotted up my path half an hour later. It was a damp, gloomy morning, the crystal landscapes of our beautiful and chilly corner of Yorkshire having been replaced by the drab tones of sodden pavements and heavy clouds. Still, I pasted on my *oh-how-lovely-to-see-you* smile, and kept my fingers crossed my masterplan would help my cause.

'Ooh, something smells nice,' John said the moment he had stepped over the threshold.

'Pastries,' I trilled. 'Just warming through.' It was a cheap shot, but you did what you had to.

'My, Casey, you certainly know how to treat us, eh, ladies?' Sophie and Kathy murmured their agreement. He then gave me a surreptitious, sideways, knowing glance. *Yes, of course I have a game plan*, my eyes said in return.

In contrast with the pastries, which had cooled down before anyone so much as glanced at them, the conversation itself soon became heated.

'No it's absolutely *not*!' I found myself saying – almost shouting – not ten minutes in. Certainly with enough vehemence to make Sophie jump. It just burst from my mouth without any conscious bidding in response to Kathy Heseltine's predictable assertion that 'After long and careful consideration of all the facts here, we have decided that it's best to move Bella elsewhere as soon as possible.'

Yes, I'd known it was probably coming, and many times, in many meetings, I had simply given my own agreement, even if it had been with a heavy heart. But not in this case. I just *had* to fight it.

'How will it help her?' I went on. 'If it's to keep her safe, I can do that. I can do that with my eyes shut. If that silly woman, or anyone else, came to the house, they wouldn't get near Bella anyway. She already knows not to go to or answer the door. Which is set locked at all times, and has a spy hole, to boot. And *obviously* I would call the police immediately.'

'I appreciate what you're saying, Casey,' Kathy said, nodding, 'but even if that were so, it would still be upsetting for her. And as we now know, which we do, that Adam Cummings doesn't have a sister, we also know she's lying, and we have a *duty* to protect Bella.'

'Have you manged to speak to him now, then?'

'Not us,' Kathy said, 'but the police have, yes.'

'And who does he think it might have been? I assume they asked him that?'

Kathy nodded. 'And he says he has no idea.'

'*Really*?' I couldn't keep the needle out of my voice.

'They think a girlfriend,' John added. 'Which would be why he's not about to incriminate her, is he?'

'Great choice of girlfriend,' I muttered irritably. 'Anyway, for what it's worth, I think you're right. Bella told me she'd thought about who it might be and mentioned some club he'd been going to a lot. She wondered if he might have met her there.'

'What kind of club?' Sophie asked.

'She didn't know,' I told her. 'But she didn't think a sports club. So maybe a book club? A darts club? A knitting club?' There was no need to point out the blinking obvious to any of them – that the woman who'd come to threaten me didn't look the type to go to any of them. I leaned forward in my chair. 'But look, Kathy, what about our *other* duties? Our duty to ensure she feels settled and happy? Our duty to enrich her life while she's taken away from all she finds familiar? Our duty to encourage her to talk about her feelings, to help her process what's happened? To talk about that *night*.' I left what I hoped was an emphatic pause. They all knew that the security benefits of billeting her with a new family would need to be set against the likely damage to her emotional health. 'We've been making *huge* progress with her just lately,' I went on. 'And I am quite sure it would be detrimental to her well-being to move her to yet another stranger's house at this crucial time.'

I shut my mouth. I had said all I wanted to on the subject. There wasn't a great deal more to *be* said. It was a simple choice – between the risk to her physically and the risk to her emotionally. I clasped my hands together in my lap. There were actually shaking. I didn't look in John's direction. I didn't dare to. Not until I heard him clear his throat.

'I have to say, Kathy,' he said, 'I'm a little surprised that we can't leave Bella here myself. I mean, yes, there *is* a slight risk, obviously, but can we not do a risk assessment first? Take a look at it all again? And couldn't we perhaps monitor the situation on a daily basis and see how things go from there? Would that be a possible solution?'

'I think that's an excellent idea, John,' Sophie said, surprising me. I felt a flicker of hope. So I had her on my side too. But would Kathy budge? Ultimately it was going to be her who'd take responsibility. Her shoulders that needed to be strong enough and broad enough if, God forbid, anything *did* happen to Bella. It was people like Kathy who stepped up to the front line if the press ever got hold of social-service-bashing stories, for that matter – with journalists like wolves, sniffing out the most damaging and damning – a job I would absolutely hate to have to do.

She turned and looked at Sophie. 'Can I count on you then – if we do this – to do a thorough risk assessment with the Watsons?' *Yes*, I thought. *Yesss.* 'And I will need to be able to count on *all* of you in this. To be extra vigilant and report even the tiniest threat. I can't emphasise that enough, I really can't. Is that understood?'

I nodded like a schoolchild promising to be good for a head teacher. I think we all did. And only just stopped myself doing a Tyler fist pump. 'Right, that's settled then. For now, Bella can remain on a strictly day-to-day basis and we will use careful monitoring to assess the situation daily at first, and then … well, all we can hope is that her long-term plan can be sorted sooner rather than later, so she can at least find out what her future holds. Which I recognise might be optimistic, given that we don't even yet have a trial date, but, well, we all want the same outcome here, don't we? For this period of purdah for the poor girl to be over. And I happen to agree with you, Casey,' she said, turning to me, 'that, the risks notwithstanding, being with you is the best place for her right now. Let's hope nothing happens to put that in jeopardy.

Particularly with everything else you have going on. Sophie tells me Bella's to be a flower girl at your daughter's wedding next weekend?'

It seemed hardly credible, but as she said that I had a major revelation. I hadn't thought of Riley's wedding once since I'd got up.

Her wedding *that was in a week*.

Now I seriously had to think of nothing else.

Chapter 15

It was the first Saturday of March and it was the big day. *The* big day. The day my lovely daughter was getting married to her David, and the weather just could not have been any kinder to us. Despite the chill and snow of the previous month, this day had dawned sun-kissed and cloudless. It really couldn't have been a more perfect day for a wedding, and Riley – who'd phoned at dawn, just to scream 'Look out of the window!' at me – was over the moon, and full of the usual delightful nonsense about how this was nature's way of apologising for it not having been on Valentine's Day.

Not that Riley had much time to spare for whimsical bridal musings. There was a to-do list, this day as any day, and, item by item, it had to be gone through.

Though this was by no means going to be a traditional wedding. Since she lived with her betrothed, as did their three children, of course, being parted on the eve of the wedding meant one of them shipping out – so she'd booted him out to spend the night at his parents, so he wouldn't see her in her wedding dress till they got to church.

And, unless you counted my sister Donna, my niece Chloe and the staff from Truly Scrumptious, there were no expensive caterers either. Instead, knowing my sister, they would have been up long before dawn, busy preparing the buffet they were going to be delivering to the local hotel where the reception was to be held.

The entertainment, too, was a pleasingly low-outlay option, as one of David's workmates was a fiddler in a bluegrass country band, no less, and he had managed to secure them for the whole afternoon at a knock-down price. I couldn't wait. I might have been denied sufficient access to my Christmas karaoke machine, but here, finally, was a chance to throw some moves, safe in the knowledge that no one could stop me. Because as far as I was concerned, embarrassing the kids was one of my chief responsibilities.

One among many. 'Right,' Riley said now. 'We need to tick everything off.'

'We?'

'Oh, Mother, *stop* it. Okay, *you*. So. Did you remember to double check that all the flowers were going to the right people?'

'Yes, love,' I said.

'And you're picking the hairdresser up at nine to bring her round to me?'

'Yes, love,' I said.

'Dad knows how to do his and Tyler's ties properly, doesn't he? Because they're not just normal ties, remember.'

'Yes, love,' I said.

'Our Kieron and Lauren know where to sit in church, don't they?'

'Yes, love,' I said.

'But are you sure? He didn't turn up to the final practice, don't forget.'

'Yes, love,' I said.

'The heating! The heating! Did you remember to remind father Brennan about the …?'

'*Yes*, love!' I said. 'Sweetheart, just chill out, will you? Everything is sorted and going to plan. In fact, why don't you pour yourself a small glass of that champagne I popped in your fridge last night? You sound like you need it. Then put it back again. I'll be round for mine in an hour.'

'Right,' she said, giggling (was she already on it?). 'I'll do that. That's a very good idea. Oh, and Mum?'

'Yes, love?'

'No one says "chill out" these days.'

I hung up and turned around to find Bella standing behind me. 'Is Riley excited?' she asked as she opened the cereal cupboard and pulled out the box of chocolate crispies. She held them up hopefully and I nodded that she could have them. It was a chocolate crispies kind of day, after all.

'*Beyond* excited,' I said. 'Which is entirely as it should be. Now then, sweetie, do you remember all our plans for this morning?'

Bella grinned at me. 'Tyler said I have to call you sergeant major and salute you if you give me any more instructions, Casey.' She duly executed a heel click and salute. Then she put the cereal box down and listed them on her fingers. 'I'm having breakfast, then a shower, then putting on my trackies, then me and you are picking up the hair and make-up lady, then we're going round to Riley's to get ready, and I'm helping Marley Mae get into her flower-girl outfit.'

'Oh, did he now?' I huffed, rolling my eyes at our slumbering insurgent. 'Well this sergeant major is about to go order that particular little soldier out of his pit,' I said. 'The cheeky sod!'

The morning passed as the mornings of weddings generally do, in a happy but focused blur of hairspray, pins and petticoats, with a soundtrack of corks popping, glasses clinking and laughter; the air fragranced by perfume and the smell of baking pastries.

Bella slotted in seamlessly and perfectly. It was almost as if she was an integral part of the family, which is entirely what every foster carer hopes will be the case. And she was an absolutely godsend when it came to the little ones, bridging the gap between frazzled grown-ups, trying to keep over-excitement to a minimum, and little girls who'd been slipped into yards of net and lace, and who, though looking angelic, were little devils fit to burst.

As for me, well, I kept having to have my make-up touched up, because every time I looked at my beautiful daughter – my precious first born – in her antique ivory wedding dress, I burst into tears.

Weddings come in all shapes and sizes, of course. And almost everyone has their own family-wedding anecdotes to share – some good, some bad, some (the very best kind, of course) so ugly they become classics on YouTube. Riley and David's – well, much as everyone loves a juicy wedding anecdote (the snapped heel, the flooded marquee, the face-off between the mother-in-laws), there was very little that wouldn't simply melt into our memories as one of those 'hug yourself' happy, happy days. And in a day that really couldn't have gone any more perfectly, Bella ended it by putting a little extra icing on the cake.

I'd hardly seen her at the reception; so fully immersed was she in the occasion that it was more the odd snapshot, of her laughing, of her showing her dress off, of her dancing with Dee Dee, of her having stepped out of her own traumatic life for the day, and having what looked like an extremely good time.

And, like the other children, to an extent that my mother even remarked on it.

'Look at them,' she said, as we took a much-needed breather from dancing. 'They look like Fagin's gang from *Oliver*, don't they?' They did, too. It wasn't a huge wedding, so there were only about fifteen children, all told – the grandkids, of course, a small smattering of nieces and nephews, plus the children of Riley and David's closest friends – but, as with most weddings, they had that special talent for inter-family intermingling; where the adults traditionally took their time to let their hair down, the kids had got together even before they'd finished throwing confetti, and were now marauding round the reception venue as a single, cohesive mob, no doubt getting up to all sorts of mischief. And Bella was very much a part of it.

And it had clearly borne fruit. 'Casey,' she whispered to me, when we were finally driving home, 'can I tell you something?'

We were both in the back of our own car now, Mike and Tyler up front, the pair of them chatting thirteen to the dozen about all the important football scores that had happened while we were otherwise engaged.

'Sure you can,' I whispered back.

'Well, you know Hannah?'

'Erm ... Hannah ... hang on. Oh, yes, you mean David and Riley's friends' daughter?'

Bella nodded. 'Well, she goes to the same school as Tyler now. And she's in year 7, like me. Did you know that?'

I told her I didn't. The last time I'd seen her, I explained, she must have been around eight or nine. 'How time flies, eh?' I said. 'Anyway, so she's there now. Well I never. So she's twelve, then, like you.'

'Not yet. Not till June.' (It always tickled me how kids knew, to the exact month, how old every other child was.) 'But she was saying how she'd be my friend if I went. And how much I'd like it there.'

'As I'm sure you would, sweetheart.'

'So I was thinking, you know, with Mum and that ... and everything ... and, like, all the work I've missed ... I think I should go back to school now, don't you?'

Chapter 16

Bella's sudden and welcome interest in returning to school galvanised me. I felt certain it was the best thing for her, not least because it would fill her days in a much more appropriate and stimulating way than I could. And with it now being March, and with Easter rushing headlong to meet us, I was anxious to get her into the local comp as soon as humanly possible. If we dragged our feet, I could see the next round of school holidays being upon us, and another enforced two weeks of trying to keep her occupied at home.

I had to press, too, because as yet ELAC (Education for Looked After Children), the body which dealt with this kind of thing, had yet to even find her a private home tutor, despite, I knew, trying their very best.

Our local ELAC officer, Paula, was at least sympathetic. I called her as soon as possible, which was the Monday following Riley and David's wedding, anxious to convey how much of a leap forward Bella's newly minted enthusiasm was.

I had a slight ulterior motive, too. We had my three eldest grandchildren camped with us for several days, and though Levi and Jackson were in school, which meant the chaos was only intermittent, we had a house full. And though this was a good thing, in that it kept Bella very, very occupied, I knew that when they left the house would feel very empty and sad. So to my mind it was vital that we didn't miss the moment; that we could slip her straight into school the following Monday, before she became all depressed again and changed her mind.

Not to mention how much I worried that if we missed the moment she would fall even further into an educational rut. 'The truth is that her mood could plunge down at any time,' I told Paula. 'As of now, she's in a place where she knows it'll be good for her, but any change in her mum's situation could knock that for six. So you can imagine how anxious I am to get her back into education right away.'

'I have it prioritised,' Paula soothed, even though she probably heard this daily, and, in reality, every looked-after child was a priority. 'And this is all to the good, to be honest, as getting the school to take her should prove a great deal easier than trying to get a tutor to come to her at home. They're like hen's teeth currently, honestly. Though there will be other factors, of course – it might well be that she'll need someone to work with her one on one for a bit, since she's been out of school so long, so –'

'I honestly don't think she'll need that,' I told Paula. She knew my background in education, so I knew she'd listen to what I had to say. 'She's a bright girl, and she's been doing work at home that her old school have been sending her. Plus going to the library. She's a proper bookworm. No worries on that score.'

'Well, I'll still mention that a TA to work with her one on one for a bit might be helpful. Might as well, eh?'

Teaching assistants often worked with children one on one for various reasons: because they had physical challenges, perhaps, or were on the autism spectrum, or sometimes, as in Bella's case, simply because they'd been out of mainstream classes for a while and needed extra support. 'Oh, absolutely.' I said. 'But if they're short of bodies, really, I think she'll be fine. She just needs to be back in school, that's the main thing,' I told her.

Paula laughed. 'Message received and understood, sir!' she said. Did I really sound that much of a sergeant major?

The weekend's fine weather had decided to be kind to us, giving a little extra help to the daffodils that were now spearing upwards in my flower beds, green and strong. And it was in the garden where I found Bella and Marley Mae, having finished my call. I thought back to what she'd told me about the night she'd spent in hers, and the sequence of events she'd spelled out to me.

Perhaps the gloomy predictions about her mum's trial were more gloomy than they ought to be. Perhaps sometime soon we'd find the key to unlock the evening that had brought her to us. Perhaps she'd find the wherewithal to sit down and tell me – us, those that needed so urgently to know – and in doing so, not make things worse for Laura Daniels, but better, in painting the full background to it all.

I'd thought long and hard about it, too. Up to now, without evidence to the contrary, from any source, the conflicts in the partnership (as far as I understood things, anyway) appeared to exist separately from Bella. There had never been any suggestion that Adam Cummings had laid a finger on his stepdaughter, or, indeed, that he had abused or neglected her in any way. Rather, it seemed the prosecution were painting an all-too-familiar picture – of a mutually antagonistic relationship between the couple, one in which Bella's mother, for all that Adam Cummings was known to be the alcoholic, played as much a part in the violent arguments as he did; started and perhaps stoked them, even. And with the feedback from neighbours seeming to corroborate that picture, why *wouldn't* she be tried for attempted murder for what she'd done? She'd bludgeoned him on the back of the head with a brick, after all, smashed his skull, and put him in a coma.

But the picture, grim as it was, was skewed; of that I was sure. The picture that was emerging, from the little bits and pieces Bella had told me, was one in which she, Bella, *was* being horrendously abused – no, not physically hit, but clearly assaulted daily by the proximity of drunken conflict, by chronic fear and insecurity, by the terror, once a row began, of what might happen to her mother, by living day and night in a kind of hell no child should have to endure. No wonder she sought escape in her books.

And I couldn't help it – call me sexist, but I refused to accept that Bella's mother was a murderess. No, I'd never met her, but I could at least put myself in her shoes. And however much it might be said that she handled things wrongly – that she shouldn't have been so quick to be the proverbial red rag to her partner's bull while her child was in the vicinity – I knew enough to know that no one *could* know how they'd deal with an alcoholic partner, especially when the well-being of a child was at risk. Who knew? Perhaps she took him on to deflect him from turning on Bella. And perhaps the strain of managing him had pushed her to her limit. Perhaps that night – who knew? – he *had* started on Bella. Perhaps that's what had made it different – made her finally snap. Perhaps she'd hit him, not to kill him, but to stop him hurting Bella. And now Bella, this bright girl, with so much self-possession, was keeping silent in order to protect her.

But *was* she helping her? Increasingly, it didn't seem so. Specially since I'd had an update from John the previous day, to let me know that Laura Daniels's lawyers were looking into the possibility of having Adam Cummings charged with a similar offence. Not attempted murder, quite – John was only hazy on the specific details – but certainly a robust response to the charges she was facing, and which had caused a renewed assault on Laura's character.

But how to convince Bella that the bigger picture might help her mum? I could only wait and listen, and hope the next interaction with Katie the counsellor – still over a week away – might bear fruit.

'What a gorgeous morning,' I said to Bella now, joining her and my little granddaughter out on the patio. 'It feels more like May than March, don't you think?'

'I love spring,' she said, tipping her head back to let the sun rest on her face. Then she turned to me. 'D'you ever grow sunflowers?'

'Not lately,' I said. 'Though our Levi did a couple of years back. It was part of a project at school. Why d'you ask?'

'I was just thinking, it'll be time to plant the seeds soon. You know, if you wanted to. You don't need pots. You just sow them straight into the ground. Two in each hole, so you can choose the best one. I was thinking you had the perfect place over there.'

She pointed to where the side fence abutted next door's shed. A distinctly sunny and sheltered spot. 'I think you're right,' I said. 'Would you like to do that? We could get some seeds from the supermarket while we're out and about on our errands later, if you like.'

'Can we?' she said. 'I'd love to do that.'

'I'd love to do that! I'd love to do that!' parroted Marley, jumping up and down.

I put my arm round Bella and gave her a hug. 'You know what? So would I.'

And I wondered if we would find ourselves measuring out her time with us in increments of growth. I wondered if she'd had that thought, as well.

On the way into town, for a round trip of shopping, seeds and library while Marley spent an hour with Lauren and Dee Dee, I filled Bella in on the state of play regarding school.

She seemed genuinely pleased. 'That's good, then,' she said. 'I won't be a dummy for much longer then. And I'll soon catch up, won't I? My old teacher at primary school said that if I'd been born in the old days I've have passed the exam to go to a grammar school.'

'I don't doubt it,' I told her. 'And you're hardly a dummy, sweetie, even with having missed a bit of school. I'm sure you'll catch up in no time. And, best of all, even if it's not your own school, it's a very, very nice one. And you know why I know that?'

'Because Tyler told you?'

I shook my head. 'Well, yes, he has, but mostly it's because I used to work there. Some of my friends still do. And I know they'll look after you. Anyway,' I said, as we reached the final junction. 'Where first? Shops and library, or library and shops?'

'Library first,' she said. 'Then we can look up the best seeds to get.'

'There's more than one kind?'

'Oh yes,' she said. 'There are lots of different kinds.'

'Well, I never,' I said. 'I didn't realise. So I've learned something today. I tell you what,' I said. 'I'm not sure you're going to need to catch up at school at all.'

Her answering beam was bright as a sunflower in itself.

Once we were both in the library, I left Bella in the reference section while I went to return the couple of books I had outstanding, then went for a browse in the new fiction section. In other circumstances I'd have happily left her there while I went to run some errands – she was twelve after all; perfectly okay to be left in a library – but the 'close monitoring' and 'special security measures' I was obliged to maintain following our visitation were never far from my mind. Though I didn't feel in my bones that Bella was in any danger from Adam Cummings's shouty 'sister', it would be negligent of me not to allow for the possibility of my being wrong. And even if it turned out that this woman was someone Bella knew (and even liked – her row was with Bella's mother, not her) any interaction with her, pleasant or unpleasant, went entirely against everything being 'in care' stood for. Any contact with anyone from her former life had to be on our terms. That was the only safe way to proceed.

And when I finally caught up with her, finding her staring into space at one of the reading tables, her expression was such that I worried that such contact had indeed taken place. I even twisted around to see if I could see a blonde head disappearing.

But it seemed not. Bella had just been poring over some weighty law books and was now staring into space because she was deep in thought.

I looked down at what she'd pulled out, dismayed.

'You know what they say about a little knowledge?' I said, as I slipped into the seat bedside her. 'It's a dangerous thing. It's why, if you're ill, looking up your symptoms is so risky if you're not a doctor. And unless you're a lawyer, I'm not sure you should be looking at books like this. I mean, you never know,' I said, aware that she was looking at me a touch irritably. (And she was right to. I had no business patronising her, and hadn't meant to.) 'You could even find something useful. But I warn you, because I've done it, that researching about the law is very complicated, and makes for very difficult reading.'

She hefted a book shut. 'I know,' she said. 'I just thought I might find something useful about when you hurt someone in self-defence.'

Was she about to open up finally? I crossed my fingers under the table.

'As in your mum hurting your dad?' I asked. Which question I knew was fine. I was just asking for context, after all.

She looked at me sharply. 'Because it was, you know. Whatever he's told the police. It really was.'

'And did you tell them that?'

A pause. 'Maybe,' she said, suddenly toneless. 'I don't remember.'

That 'toneless' bothered me. The change in her look, too. I cast a hand over the half-dozen books. 'So what did you find?' I asked lightly.

She pulled one towards her. 'That there's something called precedents. And that's what you have to find. Anyway,' she said, her expression changing again. A smile blooming as she closed a final book ready to put them back again. 'At least I found out the best sunflower seeds to buy.'

I sighed as we climbed back into the car, bound first for Lauren's, then on to pick the boys up from school. We had come so close. I knew it. But something was still holding her back. 'Something'. The word stuck in my brain. It obviously wasn't simply 'something'. It was fear. Fear of the consequences of breaking her self-imposed silence.

And all I could do was be there for when the moment eventually came when the stress of keeping it in became too much to bear. Which might not even happen – not until after her mother had been to trial, even, and the future would have been decided without her input.

I could only hope that wasn't the case, because I still felt so strongly that her testimony could only be helpful.

Right now, however, it was all about getting the kids organised and given a snack, then getting a designated flowerbed ready for its new occupants – thinking about how best to ensure it was safe from both next door's cat and, down the line, Tyler and Denver's games of football.

So I wasn't really taking much notice of the pile of post sitting on the doormat. I simply picked it up and dumped it down on the kitchen table. It was only once I'd got the children's lunch boxes washed out, and the children themselves were all outside playing, that it claimed my attention.

I was only flipping through idly – a cursory glance earlier had already told me it was mainly junk mail and a couple of utility bills – when a small handwritten envelope, hidden between the latter, caught my eye.

And I knew straight away who it was from. Same writing. Same stationery. Same sparing address. So when she'd paid her friendly visit she still hadn't noted down the house number.

Keeping an ear out for Bella, I flipped it over and worked a finger into the edge of the seal, then drew it hastily along. Inside was a single sheet, and an even shorter note than last time. Just a couple of lines, written in the same childish hand.

Mrs Watson
Please keep your nose out of what doesn't concern
you. You don't know anything about anything and you
need to remember that. DO NOT fucking slag my
brother off to the coppers, okay?

No signature. No 'concerned citizen' line, either. We both
knew that I knew who she supposedly was. I wonder what
had prompted this. How had she even come to the conclusion that I was slagging anyone off to anyone? All I could
think of was the information I had passed on to John about
Bella's Hallowe'en disclosures. She might not be his sister
but she was obviously pretty close to him if she was already
au fait with that. But perhaps it really was that simple.
That John had told Kathy, and Kathy had told the police,
and that the police had spoken to the lawyers or whoever
(the law *was* bloody complex) and Adam Cummings had
now been questioned about what had happened on
Hallowe'en night. And was now getting fretful.

I folded the letter back in half. She was clearly keen to
fight his corner. And did I think that would involve
anything more precipitous than this? No. That Bella
might come to harm at her hands at any point? No, again.

Big decisions should be made slowly, their consequences
carefully weighed. But all I could think was that if I told
John about this letter there would be only one consequence. That they would immediately take Bella away.

No other consequence seemed to take priority over that
one. Not even the possible consequences for myself. I put
the letter back in the envelope and then gripped it tightly.

The Silent Witness

Then ripped it into as many pieces as I could manage – sixteen, I think – before stepping on the pedal of the pedal bin and dropping them in.

As if it had never even existed.

Chapter 17

I felt tense over the next couple of days – as if I were living on borrowed time. And it wasn't the first time I'd felt that way, which only made it worse. Nothing like being the master of your own potential downfall to concentrate the mind.

Nevertheless, even though I initially thought 'What the hell have I just done?', as anyone sensible would, I soon dismissed the notion. I had only done what I'd needed to do.

Both in my work as a foster carer and previously when I'd worked in schools, I had sailed a little too close to the wind on a couple of occasions, and it was always for the same (and, to my mind, rational) reason. Because I was convinced I was doing the right thing.

Not that sailing that close to the wind was an easy manoeuvre, as any salty seadog would tell you. There was always a trade-off – do the right thing and risk jeopardising your job, or take the safe route on the job front and accept that you might spend the rest of your life regretting it.

Which probably sounds a bit dramatic, but that's always the dilemma, and it's my blessing and curse that when I decide something I stick to it. And even if it does make me question whether it's worth losing my job, on every similar occasion I'm afraid the answer is yes.

In any event, I only had myself to blame if the powers that be didn't see the situation in the same way as I did, because, even as I tore it up, I knew that, whatever happened as a consequence – even if it turned out to be nothing – I would at some point have to admit to what I had done. I'm not a dishonest person and I would have to open up at some point and face the consequences, or I knew it would continue to eat away at me.

As it stood right now, however, I was barely conscious of it even nibbling. No, in pride of place on my post-letter-ripping-up mental to-do list was that I had given myself time; time in which I had to get Bella to talk. Or my rash, impulsive act would have been in vain.

In that sense, my push to get Bella back into school was a double-edged sword. On the one hand, going to school might prove a positive catalyst, in that, back among peers, Bella might better visualise her future, but, on the other hand, it meant less time spent with me.

On the whole, though, I was cheerful when the call came from ELAC first thing on the Thursday – not least because Bella being safely in school meant that, should something further happen with Adam Cummings's spurious sister, chances were she wouldn't even be around.

'And it sounds as though there is plenty of scope for her to have some TA support,' added the ELAC man, who was called Howard, and sounded very posh. 'At least to take us to the Easter holidays, by which time she will have hopefully settled in. My colleague tells me she's a bright girl?'

'Definitely,' I confirmed.

'Excellent. That should make a world of difference. Hopefully her recent traumas won't have set her back too far, but you know as well as I do how often children struggling with their home lives tend to switch off educationally as well. So that's good news.'

'It is indeed,' I said. I knew all too well, from my experiences as a behaviour manager in that same school, how quickly children with emotional and behavioural problems could flounder, and if that went hand in hand – as it often did – with them struggling with their school work, it soon became a doubly destructive spiral; if you couldn't keep up, you tended to withdraw, which made it harder to contribute to lessons, which meant you fell further behind, which meant you withdrew even more, fearful of the shame and wrath of bullies.

Hopefully, not so Bella, whom Howard told me he'd be coming to visit at home the following Monday, so he could assess where she was academically.

'How about learning support?' I said, thinking of my old friend and Special Needs Co-ordinator there, Julia Styles. Though I didn't think Bella would struggle academically, she would continue to be vulnerable emotionally until there was some degree of certainty in her life – be it that she'd remain in care while her mother spent some time at Her Majesty's pleasure or, by some miracle, the process to reunite mother and daughter was begun.

'Again,' Howard explained, 'that will depend on how she does on her assessment. But we can discuss all that when I come out, of course. And am I right in thinking you have connections at the school yourself anyway?'

I told him I did, and that it made me sound like some sort of educational gangster, hustling for favours. And he laughed. I put the phone down feeling altogether more positive – and that, if my connections came good, and Bella thrived in my old comp, my little crime would be even more able to be justified.

Bella, too, seemed very pleased with the situation, even going so far, when she appeared downstairs, having had her shower and hair wash, to do a little Tyler fist pump at the news, followed by her telling me she was 'well' happy – another Tylerism.

'I'm happy too,' I said. 'I think being back in school will be good for you. And something to tell Mum about when you see her, eh?'

Which was happening today, hence the hair wash, and my promise to style it for her, and I couldn't help noticing how, one way or another, an element of hope had crept into her manner. I didn't know quite what she'd been reading in the library, only that whatever it was, she seemed to have a new handle on the situation. I just hoped that hope wasn't about to be dashed.

She nodded happily, and I thought, as I often found myself doing, about the remarkable adaptability of children. Here she was, in appalling straits, the like of which you wouldn't wish on anyone, let alone a twelve-year-old, yet there were moments, such as this one, when her stoicism astounded me. When the light of hope was sufficient – at least that's how it looked – to banish the demons into exile.

'So we'll be needing some uniform,' I said. 'Perhaps we'll all of us take a trip into town tomorrow to get you some. Right now, though, we'd better get the hair salon open for business, so you can look your very best for your visit to Mum, eh?'

'And let's hope it's for the last time,' she said. 'Oh, I *so* hope this'll soon be over and she can come home. Oh, and we mustn't forget to take the picture of the sunflowers for her,' she added. 'Well, the place in the ground where they are underneath anyway. Wouldn't it be amazing if she's home before they've grown?'

I should have known not to get my own hopes up, of course. But amid the flurry of getting ready, of Sophie's arrival, of taking the photo of the patch of neatly tilled earth with the little wooden sticks in, under which those sunflower seeds nestled – oh, and of course printing it out for her – I obviously forgot to pop my realistic head back on. But as soon as I saw Sophie's car pull up again five hours later – in what felt like a moment of *déjà vu* – it landed with a resounding whump on my shoulders.

The grandchildren had just finished their tea when they arrived – Tyler holding court at the head of the table, and, seeing Bella and Sophie climbing back out of the car, his, 'Uh-oh. Doesn't look like it went well, Mum,' took the words right out of my own mouth.

We exchanged mutual frowns. 'D'you want to take the little ones out into the garden for a play?' I asked him. He nodded sagely. He didn't need telling twice.

I went to the front door to greet them, fearing the worst. And also getting it, seeing Bella's pale face and Sophie's glum expression.

'I won't hang around,' the latter said, her hand on Bella's shoulder. 'I've got a meeting I mustn't miss and the traffic's pretty hellish. Anyway, see you soon, sweetheart,' she added, giving Bella a quick hug. 'Chin up, okay?'

We'd have a chance for a proper debrief later – I knew Sophie would send me an email – so I told her to get her skates on and waved her back to her car.

'So,' I said, turning to Bella, who'd stood on the doorstep to wave with me. 'Feeling a bit low? Come on. Let's get you a cuppa, eh? And you can tell me all about it. Tea'll keep till you've had a chance to get it off your chest.'

I half expected her to tell me she just wanted to go up to her room and be on her own for a bit, but was relieved when she nodded her agreement and followed me into the kitchen. And yet again, I felt a small jab of justification. She clearly wanted to talk. Clearly *did* need to get it off her chest. Had she been taken away, that reassuring sense of familiarity would be gone.

'I can't imagine how hard it must be for you,' I said, sitting down at the kitchen table with her. 'Seeing your mum in that place. Having to talk to her with all those people around, listening in to your conversation. But at least you've seen her. And at least she's seen *you*, for that matter. That will have helped her a lot, believe me – just seeing your lovely face, being able to hold your hands, knowing *you're* okay.'

She nodded glumly, then buried her face in her mug and sipped her tea.

'So,' I went on. 'Did you tell her all about the sunflowers you're growing? Show her the picture? Well, such as it is! But you know what, I'll bet you with all this sunshine we've been having that you'll have something to show for it, *and* to tell her about, in a matter of days. Pound to a penny those seedlings will have popped up by tomorrow.'

She nodded again, her eyes beginning to fill with unshed tears. 'But I want her to come *home*,' she said eventually. Plaintively. 'I just want her to be let out of that horrible place, and come *home*.'

I stopped myself from uttering my knee-jerk response of 'and she *will*'. Because I didn't know that. Didn't even believe that, to be honest. Not in the short term, at any rate. How on earth was that going to happen? She'd be released, if she was going to be, once the law had run its course. And the law, of necessity, moved very slowly. And it struck me that, perhaps for the first time, neither did she believe it, either. I wondered what had passed between them, but I knew I mustn't ask.

'I know, love,' I said. 'I know how hard this must all be for you. How much it must hurt to see Mum in that place.'

She didn't say anything for a moment, just put the mug down on the kitchen table and turned it around between her hands. 'I just don't know what to *do*,' she said.

'Do?'

'Do to *help* her.'

She fell silent again. I put down my own mug. Perhaps I *should* seize the moment. 'You know,' I said, 'the brain's a funny thing, Bella. And clever, too. Sometimes our brains are cleverer than we realise. Sometimes, when something bad happens – something we've seen but wish we could un-see – well, the brain has this way of protecting us. You know, shutting us off from remembering things that are too painful to remember. So the remembering of them can't hurt us even more than they've already hurt us, you know?'

She nodded, but her eyes were downcast, as if she didn't want to look at me.

'But as time passes,' I went on, 'sometimes it lets glimpses of things in through the fuzzy bits. Just little glimpses of the bigger picture. And that's hard too, because you're not sure you can make sense of what you're remembering, and then you're scared, because you're not sure you can believe what you saw …'

Bella lifted her eyes to mine, but as our gazes met she immediately lowered them.

'Because sometimes we don't *want* to believe what we saw. Sometimes we wish so hard for what we saw happen not to have happened … because it doesn't quite fit with everything else we know … doesn't fit with the bigger picture. You know, in your case, how your mum is, and how your dad is …'

Her eyes met mine again. 'He's my *step*dad.'

'Your stepdad,' I quickly acknowledged. I reached out to touch her hand. 'I understand, you know,' I said quietly. 'I know how hard it is to tell the truth sometimes, Bella. Because though it's what happened, it's still at odds with the truth – the bigger truth – that *you* know.'

A single tear tracked down her cheek and disappeared under her chin. 'Sweetheart, you're in such a horrible situation. Only you know what happened that day. Just your mum, and your stepdad – and *you*. But, you know, however much you think it'll make everything worse for your mum if you say what happened, if it *has* come back to you – even if it's just bits of it – it might help a lot if you feel brave enough to tell someone. It might help your mum. I know I can't promise that, but from what I *do* know, I think it might. Because right now,' I ploughed on – in for a penny, in for a pound … 'With your mum saying one thing and your stepdad saying another, the people who have to make all these huge, difficult decisions don't know who to believe, do they? Which is why they end up having to ask other people – friends of your mum and your dad – neighbours, whoever – what *they* think. And whatever you saw, however much you worry that it might be bad for your mum, it won't make it worse than it is all the while they *don't* know, will it?'

I could have said more. So much more. But how could I begin to even hint at what I knew about the case being made against Bella's mother? For one thing, I still felt it was a confection, at least in part. And even if there were elements of truth buried in the vitriol, what Bella had already told me put that in a very different perspective. Her mother may be no saint, but she had also been sorely tested. And if Bella didn't paint that bigger picture, who would?

And for another thing, it was absolutely not my place to lead or coerce her into saying anything. In that sense, I had already overstepped the mark.

I sat back. 'You must be exhausted, sweetheart,' I said more briskly. 'And hungry? How about some food?'

She shook her head.

'Well, perhaps you're in need of a lie-down before anything else,' I said. 'Maybe get into your jim jams, yes? Let the dust settle. No more chat from me for the moment. Come on, how about I run you a nice bath and we –'

'I want to,' she said, surprising me. 'I really, really want to tell the truth, Casey. They think I don't but I *do*. So *badly*. I hate that they're asking everyone else. What do they know about it? I *told* Sophie that.' She went silent again.

I held my hand out. She took it. 'I just *can't*.'

Because all the kids were around, and I had no right or wish to banish them (or, indeed, scuttle off and go into a marital huddle), I had to hold off the summit talk and debrief I really wanted to have with Mike. Instead, once the little ones were in bed, I sat in front of the TV (Bella having decided on an early night in the company of her favourite wizard) where all I could do was sit and half-watch the television while having the conversation with myself.

How bad had it been? That was what I kept coming back to. How bad could it have been that she dare not – would not – voice it? Despite all of my years studying children, of reading up on behavioural therapy and psychology, and working with troubled kids, I had absolutely no clue how I was going to help unlock the secrets this child was keeping. And until someone did, be it me, or her counsellor, or Sophie, or anyone, we were all floundering about in the dark.

And for the first time I had to seriously entertain the thought that maybe her stepdad *was* the one telling the truth. That, contrary to everything I believed, he had done nothing to provoke the attack by his wife. That his story – of drinking heavily, falling asleep, of waking up to find himself being violently attacked by his partner – *was* the truth.

Was Bella just doing exactly what her mum had told her to? Pretending to have seen nothing because that same mother had told her that if she told the truth she wouldn't even *have* a mother, not physically, at any rate, and potentially for years and years.

I didn't need Mike to speak to hear his voice in my ears. Perhaps that *was* the truth of it, and it was giving me one hell of a headache.

Mike and I were still sitting in front of the telly, Tyler playing a game on the laptop, when Bella reappeared. Woken from a doze, I looked at the clock, and was surprised. After our conversation I'd made a point of going up and checking on her an hour earlier (and the little ones, who'd taken over Ty's room – he was stoically camped out in the conservatory for a few days), and at that time she'd apparently been sound asleep. But something had now woken her. Upset her. Perhaps a nightmare. Hardly surprising, given the sights, sounds and emotions her memory bank was probably now filled with.

Seeing Tyler acknowledge her, I turned around to see her standing there in her dressing gown, her faithful Dobby hanging down from her hand at her side. I could tell from her puffy eyelids that she'd been crying.

She didn't speak, but it was obvious she needed me to go to her, so I got up immediately and herded her across the hall and back into the kitchen, where I sat her down once again, on one of the kitchen chairs.

I then plucked some kitchen roll from the holder, pulled out another chair and sat across from her, so our knees were almost touching. I handed her the kitchen roll, which she put in her lap along with Dobby. Now I'd sat her down, I realised she was, in fact, dry-eyed. That whatever crying she'd been doing was now over.

'What's up, love?' I asked her. 'You getting stressed about what we talked about earlier? Or is it school? Have you got the jitters now? Because, you know, it's –'

'No, it's not that,' she said, folding the kitchen roll into squares. 'It's just that I've been going over and over things ...'

'Things with Mum?' I asked gently.

She nodded. 'Casey, can I ask you something?' she said.

'Course you can. Anything. You know that, love.' I waited.

'It's just that ... what d'you think is worse? Is it worse to break a promise or is it worse to tell a lie?'

Philosophy, then, no doubt related to our chat earlier on. 'Can't,' she'd said. Can't tell the truth. I re-ran the question in my head, putting it in context. A promise or a lie? I felt a prickle at the back of my neck. Was this going where I thought (and hoped) this might be going? 'Hmm. That's a tricky one,' I said.

'It's not a trick question, honest.'

'No, I know that, love,' I said, reaching out to squeeze her arm. 'It's just a hard one so I'm going to need time to think about it. Hmm .... I suppose it depends. On what the promise is you might be breaking. And on what the lie is.' I leaned closer. 'Can you give me a little more to go on?'

Clearly not. Her response was a small but unmistakable shake of her head.

'Ok-ayyy ...' I said. 'Fair enough. But, well, in that case I can only answer you hypothetically. You know that word?' Bella nodded. I bet she probably did, too. 'And I think you'd have to ask yourself what the consequences might be – you know, of breaking the promise as opposed to telling the lie. And who you made the promise to, of course. I suppose that's the main thing, isn't it?' I went on, beginning to settle into my thinking, but still conscious of my responsibility not to lead her. 'That and how big a thing the promise is. You know, sometimes we're asked to make a promise to someone and, because it's someone we care about, we immediately say yes, don't we?'

I paused for a response, and was rewarded with a small movement of the head. 'And, sometimes, we make that promise without really thinking what it might mean for us. Us *or* them. And that's because sometimes we don't know what the consequences might be. We don't have crystal balls, do we? So it's not clear-cut. If you make a promise and then realise you shouldn't have, for either your or the person you made the promise to's sake, then sometimes you have no choice but to break the promise. And, when it comes to a lie ...' I paused again. She was looking at me so intently, I felt I had to think about every word. 'Well, we've already talked about white lies, haven't we? Remember? When we were talking about Facebook the other week? Almost all of the time, though, telling the truth is the only right way to proceed, and that's not just because you should tell the truth, because it's the right thing to do – it's almost as important because when we tell a lie it lives on inside us, doesn't it?'

I touched my chest, remembering that letter I'd binned, and thinking, *Ain't that the truth?* But was my doing so about to be vindicated? The fact that she was still here, sitting opposite me, asking me questions of moral philosophy. Would this be happening if she'd been taken from us and was now in another stranger's home?

Since she was showing no signs of doing anything other than listen, I ploughed on. 'That's the thing about lies. They're a bit like rust on a new car – eventually, just like rust, lies begin to corrode you. Because telling one lie so often means you have to tell *more* lies. So, on balance, I'd say, with very few exceptions, that it's always the better choice to tell the truth.'

I sat back a little. Bella did as well. And then spent a few moments seemingly in silent communion with Dobby, the kitchen roll now a small piece of origami in her lap. Then she looked at me again. 'Yes, but which is *worse*?'

Ah. A good point, I hadn't actually answered that one, had I? I leaned forward again. 'Sweetheart, that's just so hard for me to say without knowing what the promise was. What the lie was. How big they both were.'

'Yes, but what if they were both big?'

She clearly needed an answer. And I was clearly expected to provide one. 'Okay,' I said, 'so if you put me on the spot, then I'd say telling a lie is usually worse. If you break a promise for a good reason, the other person will usually understand if you explain to them, because we make promises to people mostly because we want to help them, don't we? Or to be kind to them. Or to encourage them ... that kind of thing. But if we tell a lie, it's more often because *we* want to get away with something, to make bad things better for *ourselves* ... Or, if for someone else – if someone asks us to tell a lie *for* them, we often know it's because they want us to help *them* get away with something, don't we? So ...'

She was nodding now, so much so that I was at pains to qualify my reasoning. 'But that's not in *every* case, sweetie. Because every situation is different, isn't it? So –'

'It's okay,' she said, gathering Dobby up against her chest in a way that made it obvious she was ready to go back to bed. She pushed the chair back. 'Thank you.'

'Well, now,' I said, 'I'm not sure I've been very helpful ...' I stood up too. 'Anyway, shall I take you back up to bed? Tuck you in?'

Bella shook her head. 'It's okay,' she said. '*I'm* okay. I can take myself up.'

And on that solemn note, she proffered a cheek so I could kiss her goodnight for a second time, then led the way out of the kitchen and took herself off up the stairs.

I stared after her for some time, wondering quite what had just passed between us. Something important, I decided. We had definitely reached some sort of watershed.

Which was good. Even so, as I returned to Mike and Tyler, I couldn't help this nagging sense that I'd said the wrong thing.

That I had *got* it wrong. That I somehow disappointed her.

Chapter 18

Bella seemed to retreat after that. No, she hadn't become withdrawn or uncommunicative or otherwise 'off' with us or anything. If anything, she was chirpy; particularly about school, where, hopefully, she'd be off to in a matter of days.

No, it was more that she had seemed to draw a line under the conversation. And all I could do was watch and wait.

The sense that I'd said the wrong things to her that night persisted, even so, and my brain was exhausted with trying to re-run my thinking, wondering how would one of the great philosophers have answered her question. In the end I could only 'park it', as Mike had suggested. What would be – where the whole family were concerned – would just *be*. Enough people were already engaged in the business of deciding what was going to happen, and it was pointless me trying to be one of them. To care and protect, that was my part in the equation. Just that. No sleuthing.

The ELAC tutor, Howard, turned out to be exactly as I'd pictured him. Very posh, very jolly, very bright. Though I didn't sit in on their session together, I could see when they emerged that they had got along famously. Howard wore a pair of very distinctive spectacles, I noticed. I wondered if he was a Harry Potter fan.

'Next Monday, then,' I commented, as Bella and I waved him off. We'll have to get our skates on with that uniform, then, won't we? Oh, and I'd better call Katie and rearrange your counselling appointment too. See if she can fit you in after school instead.' I shut the front door. 'So. Excited?'

'I am, actually,' Bella told me. 'I'm looking forward to seeing Hannah again. But Casey?'

'Mmm?'

'You know, I don't really think I *need* to see Katie any more.'

Appearances can be deceptive, however. Just as the swan, which seems to glide over the water so serenely, hides the furious, focused paddling that goes on underneath, so Bella's self-possession hid a maelstrom inside.

Which we might not have even known about – might not have even surfaced before she left us – had it not been for a trigger from an unexpected source – namely her watching TV with Tyler.

It was the following evening, which was unremarkable, just a regular weekday night. Well, except that, for one night only, Lauren and Kieron were hosting the little ones to give us a break.

And I'd used it well. The uniform had been bought, and Katie's appointment had been rearranged. (Despite Bella's assurance that she was no longer in need of counselling, I had decided to overrule her. Counsellors were rare commodities, and I wasn't about to relinquish this one.)

Mike was out – he'd gone with a mate to a local football league meeting (at the pub, of course) – and while Tyler and Bella sat in front of the telly, one at either end of the sofa, I was doing a bit of light internet shopping.

I was just price-checking a summer dress when a change in the room hit me. They'd been watching an episode of *CSI*, and up to now they'd been chatting quietly as well.

Tyler did love his crime, and this series particularly, which followed the life and times (and grisly murder investigations) of a group of crime scene investigators in Vegas, so much so that he had Mike record the late-night editions so that he could watch them uninterrupted when there was nothing else on.

But this was their third in a row – I had long since grown restless – and it looked like they might be getting a little too engrossed, and it occurred to me that, since Bella didn't need any further fuel for nightmares, it should also be their last.

'That's it after this one, guys,' I said, looking across to them. 'We've seen enough of the Vegas team for one night, I think.'

Tyler instinctively put a finger to his lips. I'd obviously spoken across something vital. But then he nodded. He valued his freedoms. 'There's only about 15 minutes left of this one, then you can watch what you want, okay?'

'Very gracious of you, I'm sure …' I began, but then realised my mistake. There was obviously something way more important going on on-screen. Abandoning the dress for a moment, I also listened.

I had either taken in more of this particular episode than I realised or, more likely, seen it before. Either way, the facts of the murder came straight back to me. The gist of the episode was that the team was at its wits' end. A man had clearly killed his wife, but there was no physical evidence that placed him at the scene, and without that or a confession there could be no trial. Grissom, the lead CSI, had consequently gathered the whole team in his office.

We could now see a bunch of photographs splayed out on his desk, the visual record of a particularly tragic murder. He pointed at each photo in turn. Then, as he usually did, which was why it had become so famous, he uttered one of his most immortal phrases. 'We need to go back and revisit the scene,' he instructed. 'The truth is there. We just have to find it.'

I rolled my eyes. It was just so formulaic. This, of course, was where they would all troop back and do exactly that, and suddenly 'see' something that had completely eluded them before.

And that was, predictably, exactly what happened. And as the case was closed and the culprit put behind bars, I laughed. 'I bet you two could have solved that way before they did,' I said.

'Course I could've,' Tyler said. 'I'm the don at detecting.'

I wasn't entirely sure what he meant by that – new words popped out of his mouth all the time these days, but while I laughed I became aware that Bella wasn't. She was still staring at the screen, in fact, watching the credits scrolling, and it occurred to me that, however much she professed to enjoy it, perhaps *CSI* was a bit close to the bone for her.

'Turn it over, Ty,' I said, nodding at the remote. 'The news is just about to start and I want to catch it.'

Tyler groaned but changed the channel. 'Bor-*ing*,' he said.

'That's as maybe,' I said, 'but it's Bella's bedtime anyway, and haven't you got some reading to do?'

Tyler was knee deep in a geography project for his GCSEs, and getting him to adopt a sensible 'one page a day' strategy for completing it was proving less than successful. 'Ye-*es*,' he began, miming a person with the whole weight of the world on his shoulders as he stood up. 'But before that –' he looked across at Bella, presumably for consensus over some delaying tactic or other. Then looked at me. And I at him. She'd gone deathly pale.

She was as white almost as the proverbial sheet, in fact. And sheeny. It was a look I was familiar with. One that suggested she might soon be sick.

And, just as I thought that, she stood up, wobbling slightly, clapped a hand to her mouth and fled the room.

Tyler stared after her. 'Stay here, Ty,' I told him. Then followed her urgent footsteps into the downstairs cloakroom.

Bella was already throwing up when I reached her, and I did what any mother would. Gathered her hair into a ponytail which I held aloft with one hand, while gently rubbing her back with the other.

She heaved several times, though there was little inside her – it had been quite a while since we'd eaten our tea – and once she stopped, I flushed the loo, put the cover back on the seat, and swivelled her round to sit down on it.

'Lord, where did *that* come from?' I asked her, noting the improvement in her colour, as I ran the cold tap and wrung out a flannel to wipe her face.

I didn't expect much in the way of an answer – she looked as surprised as I did – but then her face began to contort in obvious anguish and pain.

'I can't do it,' she managed to splutter at me, through deep, gasping breaths. 'I can't. I just can't.' Another heaving, heavy sob. 'I've got to tell the *truth*. I just can't *not*. She'll go to prison *for ever!*'

I handed her the flannel, which she took, and pressed hard against her face, her shoulders moving rhythmically as she wept.

I squatted down in front of her, gently held her wrists and pulled her hands away. 'Time to talk,' I said, 'okay? Time to get this all outside of you. Come on. Tell you what, let's take ourselves off to the conservatory, shall we? Come on, love,' I finished, taking the flannel from her. 'Time to let it go.'

She didn't move at first, just stared sightlessly in front of her, her eyes glazed, her cheeks growing pink. But when

I held out my hand to her, just as I'd done when she first came to us, she looked down, acknowledged it and took it.

Finally, I thought, though with no sense of satisfaction. Finally, we were going to learn the truth.

Chapter 19

It had been a hard day at school, that day. So much harder than she'd imagined it would be. One of those messy end-of-term days she'd always enjoyed at primary school, but which had turned out to be anything but fun.

She missed primary school, still. Missed it badly. She missed her kindly year six teacher, Mrs Huggins, who'd said 'You'll be okay, you will, missy' to her, over and over again. 'You're bright.' Mrs Huggins often said that to her too. Whispered it, in fact, as if it were their special, guilty secret. If only she could understand exactly *how* that would make things okay. Being good at schoolwork didn't *change* anything, did it?

Mostly, she missed the routine. The sameness. The security. The knowledge that school was a place where almost everything was predictable, where things were done for reasons, where nothing ever changed. Where she was safe. Where she always knew where she was, and where she should be. Where violent outbursts were the exception rather than the norm.

She particularly missed the silence of the primary school library. The tiny library in her old school had become her refuge in all the madness. The place where she could be assured of a warm, enveloping hug – of the sunshine spilling down on her, always sprinkled with dust motes, as she'd sit cross-legged with an atlas or nature book on her lap. The big high school library, which she'd sought out as soon as she'd started there, had not been the same. It was a place of hidden corners. A place where older girls schemed and bitched and giggled and where, one time, she'd come upon a boy and a girl kissing. And more. And who'd told her to fuck off.

There'd been chocolates, she remembered, at previous Christmases. Chocolates wrapped in coloured foil. An end-of-term treat. She remembered Mrs Huggins handing the tin round; the tin with the snowy scenes of Victorian skaters stamped on the outside, the inside full of multi-coloured jewels. Take two, she'd told everyone. It's Christmas! Happy Christmas! And Bella had chosen thoughtfully, her hand hovering over favourites; a yellow one, finally, and an emerald green. And she *had* had a happy Christmas. Well, for the most part, at least. It had all got so much more horrible since then.

It was a long day, that end-of-term day, despite the teachers' so obvious wish for it to be over. They rolled their eyes, all the teachers at her new, scary high school. Talked – joked, even – about the 'lunatics taking over the asylum', barked warnings about 'nonsense' and 'stupidity' and 'detentions', and issued threats about next term coming around all too soon.

Even so, despite the cartoon they had democratically agreed to watch in their year seven form room, there was this growing sense of anarchy beyond its walls. Shouting, running, swearing, the sound of chairs tumbling and doors slamming. High school was a big, frightening place when you were eleven; where year eleven boys routinely stalked the corridors like angry giants, their acne like eruptions of malevolence, seeping from their faces. Where a year eleven boy was often as big and as powerful as a grown man.

That day, despite everything she knew she'd be going home to, Bella couldn't wait to get home.

Had that been it, partly? That she'd fooled herself so completely? That, because it was nearly Christmas – if you believed the carols, a time of goodwill to all men – she'd expected something different? That her mum and her dad would be somehow different? That her dad wouldn't shout and her mum wouldn't scream, and the spirit of Christmas, even if she didn't believe in Father Christmas, would somehow make it all go away?

The school bus had, thankfully, been half empty. It wasn't a school bus as such, just the bus that happened to pass the high school at the right time of day. Anyone could use it, but very few who didn't actually go to the school did. Who would, if they had the choice of getting another, more civilised one, after all?

But today, because so many of the older kids had bunked off the afternoon, the journey through the sleety drizzle – that looked nothing like snow – was a still time, a quiet time, and she made it home unmolested; no jeers from the 'popular' girls, which she'd learned were a particular tribe there. No 'accidentally but on purpose' being bumped by backpacks.

But then she'd turned into their road and the first thing she'd noticed was that the fairy-light net her mum had draped over the bush in the front garden wasn't flashing its welcome, the way it had done since the previous weekend, when they'd put it there. The 'Santa Stop Here!' sign was also missing.

She'd been in two minds about the sign, because she was really too old for it, but it was only from the pound shop and her mum wanted her to have it. 'You're never too old to make a wish, B!' she'd said.

Bella wished now. Wished the fairy lights into sudden, winking brilliance. Which might yet happen; they worked on solar power, and it was only just properly dark now, after all. And then she saw the sign – well, half of it, anyway. Lying splintered in the middle of the road.

Bella wished again. That what she knew had happened *hadn't* actually happened. That the evidence of her eyes was telling her lies. But wishes didn't tend to come true, despite what her mum always said. The proof was there, in the front garden, which was a sorry-looking garden. (An embarrassment to the whole street, one of their neighbours had once said.)

There it was. The top half of the 'Santa Stop Here!' sign, and strewn close by, in the dirt, was the net of Christmas lights. And she wanted to run then. Run all the way back to primary school. To Mrs Huggins, who had never said, but Bella knew had an inkling, and maybe more. She wanted to run all the way back to primary school and tell her all of it. Perhaps then she'd learn how Mrs Huggins knew she'd be all right.

But she couldn't do that because she had to help her mum. Who – she'd said it to Bella again, and again, and again – had to help her dad because he couldn't 'help himself'. Her *stepdad*. She'd been thinking a lot about that lately, after spending almost her whole life not ever thinking about it at all.

But how could you not think about it when it was spat into your face? Didn't matter how many times her mum had told her he didn't mean it, he did. He had. Because he'd said it to her, hadn't he? And you just didn't joke about stuff like that. And her mum hadn't been there, so she didn't know *how* he'd said it. How he'd yelled at her. 'Fuck off out of my face, you little brat!' And she'd said, 'Stop it, Dad! Stop it!' and then he'd turned round and just said it. Raised a fist, too, even though he'd never hit her before – he only did that to her mother – and said, 'And I'm not your fucking dad! Got that? You GOT that?'

He hadn't hit her. She didn't think he ever would, for some reason. But then again, he hadn't really needed to.

She'd shrugged off her backpack, placing it on the doorstep rather than the wet garden, and spent some time trying to sort out the stricken fairy lights, draping them once again into place over the sodden bush. To make things better. Make things right. To put off going inside, mainly.

But it was hopeless. The solar sensor was face down on the damp ground. And had obviously been lying there a while. She put her hand over it, and was rewarded with a faint glow from the LEDs, but with the scant daylight they'd had, all of it cloudy and sleet-soaked, she knew they were all but expired. She pushed the spike back into the ground and set it up for the morning anyway. At least tomorrow night they would light up, which mattered.

There was nothing to be done about the sign, though, so she ignored it. And with little in the way of options – their mostly old neighbours were mainly horrible, not like the friendly, twinkly-eyed ones you always read about in children's books – she picked up her backpack, retrieved her newly minted, high-school girl's door key, weighed it in her hand and slipped it into the lock on the front door. Happy Christmas, she thought, smelling beer.

The house was silent, momentarily, and her first feeling was relief. Whatever had happened was obviously long over. With any luck, her dad would have stormed off to wherever it was he had taken to storming off to lately – he didn't seem to be working much, but he was forever storming off these past few weeks. And the lights and sign – evidence of a tantrum? (her mum often called the things her dad did 'tantrums') – seemed to suggest that was the case. But you never knew. Equally, they could be out in the back garden. But then she'd hear them, surely? They were always so, so loud.

She often wondered about that, about how alcohol always raised the volume. About why it made everyone shout so much louder – not just more angrily, but with such enormous volume. That and how her mum, who always spoke so quietly (who did everything quietly, 'so as not to wake the beast' – she'd often tell Bella that, creeping around the house like an apologetic wraith), would raise her own voice to match his, once a row had got going, like their voices were swords, trading thrusts and blows.

But the silence was broken, as her instinct had already told her it surely would be, though not by a shout, but a drumming, scuffling sound. A sound coming from the back room – the room that in other houses would normally be the dining room, but in which they never 'dined', or even ate. She ate her tea most days on a tray on her lap in front of the telly. The back room was essentially just a dumping ground. A dumping ground with an armchair, with blackened, greasy arms on it, where her not-your-fucking dad would sit, hour after hour, getting pissed and spilling beer froth down his front.

He'd wipe his hands on the chair arms, always. Wipe the wetness from his fingers. So they were pickled in old beer now, just like he was.

She walked the four strides down the hall, throwing her bag down as she did so, so she could investigate what was going on, because what else was there to do? Again the scuffling sound, just as she turned towards the open door – as if a dog was trying to rootle something out.

It wasn't a dog. They had no dog. She'd never been allowed a pet. Not even a goldfish. It was her mother and her stepfather, the latter on his knees, straddling her mother's middle – while she, on the floor, was on her back, stretched out beneath him, and the scuffling noise was the sound of her feet scrabbling for purchase on the wooden floor.

He had his big beery hands around her throat.

'GET OFF HER!' Bella roared. It came from deep down inside her. Closely followed by action that was instant and instinctive – she threw herself on top of the hill of her stepfather's back. He exploded backwards at her touch, knocking her straight off again, launching her painfully against the door jamb, and throwing a punch at her for good measure, which missed its mark but connected painfully with the side of her leg. He had hit her.

But at least she had surprised him. She remembered thinking that, gratefully. Feeling grateful at how she was good at creeping around too. He roared back at her, incoherently, twisting his torso, staggering upright, stepping on her mother's forearm in the process. But clambering off her, at least, to express his incoherent fury that his not-his-fucking-daughter had the nerve to take him on.

Bella's mother howled too, like a new-born who'd sucked some air in. Red, just like a baby, too, clutching at her neck. Had he actually been *strangling* her? Trying to *kill* her? Her mum was coughing now, pulling herself up, one hand still clutching at her throat. She yelled something. 'Brute' maybe. And 'Don't you fucking TOUCH her!'

Bella scrambled back up onto her own feet, her eyes fixed on her father, who was now stumbling drunkenly towards his armchair, reaching down on the floor beside it, groping for a can. Even now. Like a prize fighter, between rounds.

'You *FUCKING ANIMAL*!' Bella's mum shouted, and the first thing Bella thought about was that the door into the garden was open. The patio door that had been replaced only eighteen months previously. The door that her mum said was the catalyst (Bella had had to look the word up) for her dad getting help and going back to the AA meetings.

And a good spell. For the most part. Though it hadn't lasted long. The glass had been replaced but it hadn't lasted long. It never did. She ignored the open door, though, even though she knew the whole street was probably out listening. Instead she hauled her mother up, and helped her to her feet. There was blood in her hair. A huge pink egg on her forehead. A dark wet patch at the crotch of her jeans.

The can whistled across then, glancing off her mother's shoulder, spewing liquid and fizzing froth over both of them. 'Bitchhhhhh!' her dad yelled back, soon following the can himself, cannoning into them as he glanced off the arm of his armchair, sending all of them back to a writhing tangle on the floor.

Bella had found some sort of primeval strength. She'd cried out, aimed a punch at him, anything to stop him, really, but for all her ferocity she was too small and weak for him, winded and gasping for breath under their combined weight. Her mother was fighting back now – Bella could feel the sudden hardness of her fists and thighs and biceps – and trying to make space for her to wriggle free. 'Get the fuck out,' she was gasping. 'Go get help! Get Mr Atkinson!' The words coming out in breathless bursts.

Get her mum's mobile. That was surely the better thing to do. Not Mr Atkinson. Mr Atkinson who was one of the neighbours who hated them. Mr Atkinson who rolled his eyes at them, who moaned in the street to her mum, embarrassingly, about the 'endless, endless scenes'. Find her mum's phone. Dial 999. Get the police. Get anyone. Get someone who'd *want* to help them. Who could see that her dad – her not-her-fucking-dad – had turned into a monster. A murderous monster who once again had his prey in his hands. And who *didn't even seem to care* that his not-his-fucking-daughter was standing there, *watching him*. Her dad who was too busy, too intent, too *determined* to kill her mum.

'Bella, GO!' she saw her mum say, though she could hardly even hear it. He had his hands round her neck again and was shaking her with them. Her head was bobbing, *thudding*, against the floorboards.

Bella wasn't sure why she stepped out into the garden. Afterwards, she became resigned to the fact that she probably never would know. She had intended, after all, to get her mum's mobile phone. Except for a pure kind of fury that had engulfed her. Was that it? Was that the word? Was it fury that had propelled her? That made her forget that she was twelve and she was terrified of him? That, like her mother, she was so used to creeping around him? That, every other time, she'd have done what her mother had told her. Called help. Got a neighbour in. Watched her father crumple, seem to shrink almost, in the face of it. Listened to her mother, wanting to scream herself, hearing her excusing him. Making light. Making less of it. Saying things like 'It's not him, it's the drink'. 'It's an *illness*.' Then the tears and the apologies and the inevitable fragile truce. Before the same thing. The same drink. The same row. The same fight.

She blinked, seeing it all there. She had read *so* many books now. She knew another word, too. (There were so many more and different books in high school.) 'Sisyphean'. The never-ending, pointless, pointless task.

Was getting help going to help her? Had it helped her in the past? No, it hadn't. And it was simple. She needed to help her mum herself. If she didn't he would kill her. She could see that so clearly. Her mum's whole face told her. It was the colour of cooked beetroot. She knew the word for it. She was asphyxiating.

Soon, if she *didn't* help, her mother would be dead.

The pile of old house bricks had been there for years. The result of some stupid plan he'd had, to build a barbecue. Back in another good spell, a long time ago now. He'd got some kit, off some other builder, which was 'a bargain' apparently. Whereas, as far as she could see, it was just a box with a few bits of metal in. A bag of various bolts, a kind of grill pan, and what looked like an oven shelf. Little more. You built the actual barbecue out of your bricks and mortar. There was a sheet of instructions for how to do it, and where the grill pan and shelf went. Even though anyone with half a brain cell could have worked that out themselves.

He'd come home with the kit and instructions and her mum had been excited reading them out to her, even so. 'This goes here, see? And then we'll have a proper, built-in barbecue.' As if having a proper built-in barbecue would make them a proper family too.

'Like I need instructions? I'm a fucking brickie!' her dad had said, laughing. All those years, and here they still sat, waiting for him.

It turned out to be surprisingly heavy, the brick she plucked from the pile. Dense. Cold and sharp. Almost too big for her hand. Heavy enough, certainly, to have to be hefted with both of them. For fear of dropping it before it hit its target.

Then her mum's voice – 'Bella! What the *hell*?' – and perhaps the word 'Noooooo!' But he'd already slumped on top of her by then.

Chapter 20

Bella couldn't remember when she'd last seen her grandmother. Four years, perhaps? Five? A long time ago. She'd given her a Moomintroll book. The last thing she'd ever given her. Her face was hard to recall now, and there were no photos of her anywhere. But her 'words of wisdom' – her mum always said that with a funny look on her face – had stayed with Bella always.

Bella's gran had told Bella lots of important things when she was little. Not to pull funny faces in case the wind changed and it stayed like that. To eat her crusts, to make her hair curl (she was glad now that it hadn't; that she could choose). To mind her Ps and Qs, which meant to be on your best behaviour. To never break a promise. And to never tell a lie.

Which left Bella now in something of a quandary.

Having heard the dull thud of the house brick as it connected with her father's head, she had – to her shock, since she hadn't actually planned it – raised it and hit him a second time, just in case. And would have done so a third time had her mother not stopped her.

Not physically; she couldn't. She was still trapped underneath him. But by the power of her voice, which was shrill and hysterical: 'Stop it, B! Stop it, B! STOP IT, B! STOPPPPP ITTTTTTT!'

Bella stopped, having never heard her mum yell like that before. Not to her. To her dad, yes, but never at her. She dropped the brick, then, a mad term she'd read recently popping into her head. To drop like a hot brick. To drop quickly. In a panic.

Her mother was in a panic right now.

'Help me,' she implored now, scrabbling her arms and legs like an upside-down beetle. 'Quickly. Help get him off me. Oh, God … Jesus. Christ. Oh, God, Bella. *Fuck*.'

Close up, Bella could now smell the urine. And worse. She didn't like to even *think* about the worse. Didn't like to look at the blood she saw too now, that was seeping, dark and steaming – condensing in the cold? – from between the dark furrows of her father's greasy hanks of hair, and stickily, from underneath his head.

A mighty shove from her mum, and he flopped over on his back, groaning, where his bleeding head went 'donk' against the floorboards. His arm, as she pushed him off, slapped hard against the armchair. He made a strange sound, not quite a moan, more a sigh. Then fell silent. Had she killed him?

'Fuck,' Bella's mum said, scrabbling up to her feet again, clutching at her head. 'I need to call an ambulance. *Shit*, I'm spinning out. Get my phone. It's on the charger.' She grabbed Bella's wrist. '*Hear* me? Get my *phone*!'

Bella backed out of the room, watching as her mother

sank back down to her knees beside her father, and for a moment she worried that she was going to pass out on top of him. Her not-your-fucking-father, who lay there with his legs splayed, very still. Her mum was talking to herself, and Bella wondered if she actually even *realised* he'd been trying to kill her. 'Shit,' she was saying to him. 'Shit. You fucking *ass*hole! See what you've done? See what you've fucking done? *Shit* ...'

Bella went for the mobile, and pulled the lightning cable out of it. Wondered grimly who'd decided to call it that and why. The kitchen was warm, and she realised the oven was on. She went and switched it off, 'on auto-pilot', she thought as she did so. What might be in there? She hadn't eaten lunch and was hungry. But they needed an ambulance. She didn't open the oven door.

Never break a promise and never tell a lie.

Bear those two in mind and you'll do all right, girl, her gran had told her. Which was something she used to think about often, if not so much now. Her mum told lies, didn't she? All the time, actually. To the people at the social. To her dad. About money. To her own mum, even, on the phone, about her own dad. She told her own mum there wasn't anything wrong, all the time, then, to her, and, more often, to her dad, or herself, she called her own dad – Bella's granddad – an evil f-ing bastard.

Bella gave the phone to her mum, who looked pale, like tracing paper, and was now in the armchair, elbows on knees, face propped up in her hands. The blood – her mum's blood – was from a cut in her eyebrow. It made a line down her cheek. It made her look like a lady-pirate off

Pirates of the Carribean. Or a lady Viking even, like her own great-great-grandmother.

Her mum took the phone. But didn't punch out 999 or anything, like Bella expected her to. Instead she held it in one hand and stared at it for a long time. Then looked up at Bella, who was still standing staring at her.

'I'm all right, B, okay? *Okay?* I'm okay. I'll be fine. Are *you* okay?' She gripped Bella's hand as she said this. 'Shit … okay … right. Here's what's happening, okay?'

'Is Dad dead?' Bella asked. She hadn't exactly meant to ask the question. But out it had come anyway. He was just lying there so still. She didn't have time to wonder how she'd feel if her mother answered yes.

'No,' her mum said. 'But he's hurt.' She glanced at him, as if he might be listening. '*Badly*. B, listen carefully, okay? I need you to listen to me very, *very* carefully. I'm going to call for an ambulance. And when they get here, whatever happens, you are to say nothing, okay? Nothing. Not a word. When they ask you, you say nothing.'

'But –'

'Nothing. Just "I don't know". "I didn't see …" Stuff like that.'

'So not nothing, then?'

'Bella, listen. You didn't *see* anything. You didn't *do* anything. You don't *know* anything. You just came in, from school, and you found us, like this.'

'But –'

'Bella, this is *important*. I can't begin to tell you *how* important. You came in. You know nothing. You *saw* nothing. *Nothing*.'

'But –'

'Bella, if you don't, it will be bad for us. Understand? Bad for you. Bad for me. You must do this for *me*. I have to call now –' She lifted the phone, pressed the home button, pressed the numbers of her password with her thumb. Bella's birthday. 1011. She'd told her to memorise it. For emergencies. 'Remember, Bella. Your birthday. Ten eleven.'

'I have to call now,' she said again. Her fingers were shaking. 'Remember, B, okay? It could not be *more* important. You saw nothing. Know nothing. Came in and found us, like this. Promise me?'

Bella nodded, automatically. There was only one response when your mum said 'promise me'. You promised.

'Promise me,' her mum said again.

'Bella nodded again. 'I promise.'

And she did. But in promising to say what her mum had told her, she would now have to tell the policemen a lie. She pointed that out. Right after her mum had made the call. ('A fight … please come quickly … he's bleeding … a head injury …')

'Noooo!' her mum yelled at her. 'Don't say that! Don't *ever* say that! You were *helping* me. Don't say that. You were *terrified*. In *shock*! God, Bella …' She was sobbing now. Bella hated seeing her mum crying. Crying into her ear, clinging on to her, half in and half out of the stinking, hated armchair. Her face wet. The urine smell – and worse – really strong now. 'You must promise me, on your *life* … This could *not* be more important, Bella!'

'I promise,' Bella said again. 'Cross my heart and hope to die.' Which made her mum cry even more.

A police car came first. Bella had gone and watched for the ambulance out the front window, as her mum had told her to, but it was a police car, lights flashing, making blue and red puddles on the road.

She felt calm as she went into the hallway to open the door to them, opening it just as their fists did a sharp police knock – rat-a-tat, rat-a-tat-tat! 'Op-en-up-we're-the-po-lice!' Policemen never rang on doorbells.

They were so quick she wondered if Mr Atkinson had already called them. With the patio door open, he must have heard something, after all. Bella wished she'd tucked the broken Santa sign under the bush.

There were two of them. Big men, lots of flaps and pockets on their uniforms. Stuff stuffed in pockets, in their belts, on their shoulders. 'All right, love,' the younger one said to her, but not as a question. All right, love, in a way that said 'We're here, you're okay now', not knowing, and wouldn't know, because she'd made her mum a promise, that she wasn't in the least bit okay. Far from it. She had a lie to carry round with her now, a very heavy one.

The policemen herded her, almost, down the hall, into the back room, where her mum, obviously expecting an ambulance man, went 'Ohhhh', then crumpled downwards, as if the bones in her legs had disappeared, just like in the Harry Potter film. Bella didn't know what to say or do.

The policemen did, though, and while one reached to stop her from falling, the other sank to his knees by her still splay-legged, silent father, felt around near his face and said 'pulse'. The other, having parked Bella's mum in the armchair again, spoke into a walkie-talkie thing he wore in his chest – ambulance, yes, forensics (a word she knew) – all the while nodding at Bella in what she thought he hoped was a reassuring fashion. But it didn't reassure her, because everything was swimming in and out of focus, her mum was sobbing really loudly, and the smell was so horrible, and she had to fight the urge to run away from these huge, scary men.

'Jesus H,' the one on the floor said. 'Jesus *flaming* H.'

Then, soon – between the crying, and the smell, and the way the policemen filled the room, she wasn't clear *how* soon – there were more people, a man and a woman in broccoli-green uniforms, and another woman, an old one, who wasn't in any sort of uniform, and who kept squeezing her shoulder and shunting her out of the way. First while a stretcher was brought in (could the room fit any more in? It was getting like Mary Poppins's carpet bag), then again, as her dad – still flat, still silent, grey and limp, and now with a plastic mask on his face – was taken out on the same stretcher, into the hall and away. Then again, as the sound of a siren outside filled the air, her mother, still sobbing, still shaking, calling 'Bella! Love you, Bella!', was taken away by the two giant policemen.

Belatedly, her mind suddenly jerking back into focus, Bella realised the enormity of what was about to happen to her. That the woman who wasn't in uniform had a third policeman with her. Who was actually a police*woman*. That this was it now. That bad things were happening.

That they were now going to take *her* away as well. But to where? She felt her insides start to liquefy.

'Up to your bedroom, sweetheart, yes?' the first lady was telling her gently, at first confusing Bella, and making her heart leap – was the lady putting her to bed? Was she going to have to stay up there on her own? 'Get some bits together,' the lady clarified. Bits? What did she mean by bits? 'Night things,' the lady said, though Bella hadn't actually asked her. 'You know, toiletries and so on. Any books? DVDs you like? Toys? Some warm clothes and that, certainly. All the usual bits and bobs ...'

Bits and bobs? But it was like the lady was talking to herself. Reeling off a familiar list in her head. An image of the Child Catcher from *Chitty Chitty Bang Bang* came into her head. Would there be a cart outside, to carry her away, with bars she'd have to cling to? *You and that imagination of yours, Bella!* That's what Mrs Huggins always used to say.

And meanwhile, the policewoman was marching round, touching everything. She had gloves on. Like in hospitals. When had she put those on? Marching round, touching and checking and doing. Sniffing. Turning the lamp off. Checking the patio door. Marching off into the kitchen. Getting tape out – stripy tape, like Bella had seen on the telly. Marching round her home as if it wasn't a home. Just a place. In a police show. As if she owned it.

Perhaps she did now. For the moment. Because home was now a 'crime scene', she realised. So she duly packed – packed whatever her gaze landed on, feeling panicked. As if there was a time limit and a buzzer might suddenly go off, like she was in a game show. She packed what the lady suggested, and she packed stuff at random, but without a plan, because she couldn't really think straight. How did you pack when you didn't know where you were going? How did you pack when you didn't know how long you'd be there?

So some stuff from her drawers, some stuff from the washing pile. The stuff from the bathroom that was hers, like her flannel. The stuff that strictly wasn't, like the one tube of toothpaste. The 'family toothpaste', she thought. But what would her mum do for toothpaste? No one had asked her to 'pack a bag, love', had they? What would her mother do for clothes?

And would her dad even need toothpaste? Her not-your-fucking-dad? She could feel the dent of his big drunken thumb halfway down it. 'I'll fucking squeeze it where I fucking like, bitch!'

No more.

It had stopped sleeting when they emerged back into the front garden, where the light net still resolutely refused to sparkle. It felt cold outside. Cold enough to snow? But not at all Christmassy.

'What's going to happen to me?' she asked the lady without the uniform, who'd come in a different car to the policewoman and who led her out into the road now – no Child Catcher's cart – while the policewoman stayed behind, by herself, at their home.

Someone a few doors down was standing at their front gate, watching. Bella couldn't tell who because it was so dark. 'So bloody rude.' She could hear her mum saying it, because she said it so often. Could hear her shouting down the road, too, like her ghost was still here. 'Know me again, love? Get a bloody life!'

Bella didn't stare back. She just got in the back of the lady's car as directed.

'We're going to take you somewhere safe, sweetheart,' the lady told her, trying to help her with her seatbelt. Fussing around her, like she was six, rather than twelve, and couldn't manage on her own. She found she didn't mind at all. She knew she should – she was too old for 'Santa Stop Here!' signs, after all – but she didn't.

The lie was almost too big for her to carry, and she wished she *could* be six once more. Back in the primary school library, back to a time almost before she could remember, where bad things – truly bad things – only happened in books.

Not in *real* lives. They drove off into the night.

Chapter 21

At some point – how long ago now, I had no clue any more – I had reached across to one of the wicker chairs and tugged off the throw that was draped across it. It covered both of us, and inside it was now almost too warm. Bella was close beside me, and while I had one arm around her, she'd slung one pyjama'd leg over my own legs, which now felt stiff and hot as well.

Tyler, I knew for sure, had long since gone to bed. As had Mike, who'd barely put his head round the door, before retreating wordlessly and leaving us to it.

It had been a long time in the telling. Perhaps a real-time account, even. But Bella had still yet to finish it.

'Then I remembered,' she said, in the same toneless voice she had told me her whole story in. 'Dobby. I'd forgotten Dobby. I couldn't leave without Dobby. Just the thought of him alone up there ...'

I squeezed her leg. 'So you went back for him?'

I felt her nod against my chest. 'I made the lady turn the car round. First of all she said we couldn't. She said it was too late now, and that she'd go back and fetch him for me in the morning. And first of all I said okay. But it *wasn't* okay, was it? I sat there in her car and it was like I was having trouble breathing. Like I had asthma or something, like Ruby does – *that* bad. Except I don't. It was just because I couldn't breathe. Because it wasn't *fair*.'

'So you asked her again.'

This time a headshake against my chest.

'I didn't exactly ask her. I couldn't get any words out. I just screamed. I didn't mean to. I just couldn't stop it coming out. Though I really tried. She was frightened, I think, *and* she was driving. So she pulled over and stopped the car. I think she was shaking as much as I was. I couldn't speak at all then, when she opened the car door and tried to get me to calm down. But I couldn't breathe. It was like I was a fish who's just been fished out of a river. Just gulping. Trying to get air in. And she said – no, she almost shouted. Holding my shoulders and going, "Okay, okay, calm *down*!" like that man does in the adverts.'

'And you did?'

'Eventually. I just couldn't get my breath, so she made me do this counting thing, holding it in. I was so *scared*. And going all dizzy and my heart was, like, exploding. I thought I was going to die.'

'A panic attack,' I said.

She twisted her head and looked up at me. 'That's it. That's what the lady said.'

'Anyway, she drove you back to the house …'

'Yes. And then she had the policewoman go and get him for me. She wasn't allowed in. *I* wasn't even allowed in,' she finished. 'It was like it wasn't even my home any more.

The policewoman was outside guarding it. I had to wait in the car while the lady went and spoke to her. But she was nice. She told me he'd missed me and that it was a good job I'd come back for him. I know it's babyish,' she said. 'But I felt better then.'

And did she feel better now? That's was the big question, wasn't it?

I suspected yes. Just by her demeanour. I hoped so. As for me, I was being shaken up by a fizz of information. Of nothing any longer being what it had seemed. Twelve, I kept thinking. What was the law when you were twelve? Ten rang a bell, but twelve? Perhaps *I* should have spent time in the library.

I eased out the leg I'd foolishly tucked under me at least an hour since. I had no idea what time it was now; only that it had long since swapped being very, very late for being very, very early. I could tell just from my heavy, sticky eyelids.

My leg freed, I tried to ignore the pins and needles that were beginning their progress up it. 'Sweetheart, I have to move,' I said, pulling down the throw as Bella slid her own leg off. 'I'm stiff as a board and my shin's currently on fire.'

Bella pulled the rest of the throw off and stood up herself, helping me to get up as she did so. 'Be careful,' she said. 'I sat for hours like that once and when I stood up I had a dead leg and fell right over.'

'I'd best hang on then,' I said. 'Hope you're feeling strong ... yweeooowww! Oh, now *that's* better,' I said as I bent down to pummel it, and stamp some life back into it. 'I can stand on it okay, now, it's just – oh, sweetheart,' I said then, looking up and seeing her stricken face. I held my other arm out and beckoned, and she scooted straight into my embrace. She'd been dry-eyed for so long now – for at least the last couple of hours of her telling me her story. But I could tell that my confident diagnosis of 'better' had been short lived. It had now hit her like the pins and needles had hit me.

'I know you have to tell now,' she said solemnly, and once again the words were spoken into my chest. 'The lady told me. The lady who first took me away – *she* told me. She kept on telling me. So did the foster lady I went to first.

'That was the thing, always. That I knew that whatever I told either of them, they would have to tell. That *anyone* I told the *truth* to would have to tell. But I have to now. I know I do. It doesn't matter what my mum said. I have to tell the truth, or my mum will go to prison for ever, and I'll have to go to hell.'

'My mum will go to prison for ever.' She'd said that to me earlier. The penny dropped. Not 'I'm telling the truth *despite* it meaning my mum will go to prison for ever.' She had to tell the truth *or* her mother would have to go to prison for ever. She was telling the truth now to free her.

I sat her down again, the fire in my leg having been replaced now by an insistent thrumming in my brain. It had been her. Oh, God – why hadn't that ever even occurred to me? 'Bella, that isn't true,' I said. 'You're not going to hell, okay?'

There was a silence. I became aware of how she was clutching at my sweatshirt.

She looked up at me, her eyes brimming with a queue of unshed tears. 'But I have to go to prison now instead, don't I?'

Had it been any later, we might have been saved by the bell. My alarm, at least, set, as ever, for half past six.

As it was, there was a low noise, of the door into the conservatory being opened. And then the looming shape of Mike, moving carefully in the darkness, coming in.

I hugged her close to me. 'Bella, you're not going to prison, either. And that's a promise.'

And one I could at least make with confidence, I thought miserably. Because if it be so decided that a custodial sentence was appropriate (oh, how I wish I'd read up on that earlier) a juvenile wouldn't ever be sent to a prison. They would be sent to a 'youth offenders' institute'. Or a 'young persons' facility'. Or some other similarly un-prisonish-sounding place.

But it would be a prison just the same.

Chapter 22

I woke up completely disoriented the next day. First by the light flooding in from the gap in the curtains, and then by the sight of the clock radio beside me, which read 11.10.

Despite the lateness of the hour, I felt exhausted. But it took a full thirty seconds or so to regain sufficient consciousness to remember the events of the night before.

I groped for a note that I saw had been propped beside a mug of what was presumably cold coffee. Not so much the night before as the morning after.

The note was from Mike, who had presumably long since gone to work.

Morning, love
I thought I'd leave you to sleep! Got Tyler up and he said he'll see you after school (I gave him his lunch money) and last time I checked Bella was spark out.
Give me a ring later, after you've spoken to John.
Love M x

I flung the covers off and leapt out of bed. We were in new territory now – new and potentially dangerous, and the last thing Bella needed was to wake to an empty house. New and frightening territory. *I* was frightened. About what she might do.

My night hadn't finished when I'd finally got Bella up to her bedroom. Though she'd seemed almost eerily calm for most of the telling of her story, the final admission that she had been the one to strike the blows that had felled her stepfather had brought with it an understanding of something which I think she'd been trying to bury for many weeks. That it was she who should be standing trial for his attempted murder.

'I would have killed him, I know I would,' she had whispered between the continuing gulping sobs that kept racking her body. 'If Mum hadn't have stopped me, I'd have just kept hitting him with that brick. It was like it wasn't even me doing it. I really, really couldn't stop. I just couldn't. If I stopped he would kill my mum – that's all I could think. That he would. He was *strangling* her, Casey …' Her voice broke and the shudders overtook her once again. 'I didn't *dare* stop,' she whispered eventually. 'I couldn't let him *kill* her. Will the police come and take me away now?'

But even the most distressed person has to succumb eventually, and, a little after four, she finally fell asleep in my arms. I'd disentangled myself gingerly, as anxious about her waking up as you'd be about a new and fractious baby, but she was a dead weight, exhausted, and was soon deeply asleep.

Sleep didn't come for me, though – my mind was whirring too much. And after deciding against waking Mike – he would have to be up soon, and it just wasn't fair – I slipped quietly out of the bed I'd so recently slipped into and went downstairs, where I spent almost an hour emailing everything to John while it was fresh in my mind.

I must have returned to bed less that an hour before the alarm was set for, but had clearly fallen into such a deep sleep myself then that neither the alarm nor the shower could wake me.

I was wide awake now, though, even though I'd still had precious little sleep. It just felt as if I couldn't sleep until Bella's revelations had been acted on. But I obviously didn't need to worry about Bella herself, not for the moment. She was soundly asleep, her features unlined by anxiety. And though her face was streaked with the evidence of just how hard she'd cried, she looked as free from care as a porcelain doll.

I headed to the shower then. I knew I would feel better for it. And within half an hour, washed and fresh again, I was ready for action. And I knew the first action would be one that would present its own problems. I already knew what John would require of me once he'd read my pre-dawn email. That I explain to Bella (persuade Bella, and, with the new day, and new clarity, she might need some persuading) that the most important thing now is that she tell her story again, this time to a stranger.

This was all new territory too. I'd dealt with lots of different care situations and observed all kinds of protocols, but I'd never cared for a child who was over the minimum age of criminal responsibility and who might well be charged with attempted murder. But would she? Could that even be possible? Due process, I remembered. She'd committed a violent act and it was the state's responsibility to respond to it – and the responsibility of her own lawyers (would she be appointed one by social services?) to defend her and to hopefully see she was acquitted.

Because *surely* she would be acquitted. How could she not be? I might have missed the mark completely in terms of what had happened, but the bigger picture remained the same. They had both been driven to breaking point by Adam Cummings's alcohol-fuelled violence. The only difference was who administered the blows.

Even by the time I was dressed, Bella was still sleeping, and I wondered if, left alone, she might sleep through the day. And if so, so be it, I decided once I considered it. Anxious as I was to begin setting the record straight, an exhausted, distressed child would be no good to anyone.

It also left me space in which to properly chat to John, who'd not as yet even called me. Bless him, I thought, once I gave it a moment's thought. He'd have seen the time of my email and put two and two together. He was doubtless giving me time to cat nap too. So I phoned him. Only to find myself listening to his answerphone, and on hearing it I hung up and dialled the main office – better to know what he was up to than just sit and wait. For all I knew, he might be out of the office all day.

But apparently not. 'I'm sure he won't be long,' the receptionist told me. 'He's just been called away to deal with a report of a missing child.'

A missing child obviously trumped pretty much everyone. So I made coffee and slipped a couple of slices of bread into the toaster, the events Bella had recounted to me still swimming around in my head.

If what Bella had told me was the absolute truth, which I strongly believed it was, then one thing I had been entirely wrong about was Adam Cummings. Or, more accurately, couldn't fathom what was going on with Adam Cummings. Had he kept quiet about what happened because he too wanted to protect his stepdaughter? Perhaps. But equally it could be true that he didn't care about Bella. That seeing his wife go down for almost killing him was a win–win situation. If it were true about her various liaisons – or the possibility of her liaisons – what better way to get his revenge?

But I didn't know. I knew nothing. And it was driving me nuts. And while I'd never profess to doing such things unconsciously, ten minutes later I found myself firing up the laptop, and doing something I'd heard of, but never done before. My kids called it stalking.

I'd even heard them talking about it – my own two, plus Riley. That thing when you catch someone sitting on Facebook and checking out someone else's profile. It was, fairly obviously, not a cool thing to do. But even as I thought that, my fingers were ahead of me, and I was typing Adam Cummings into the search bar.

I was slightly shocked to find him, even so. Hadn't John said something about all parties involved deleting their social media accounts? And wasn't there some legal need for them to do so? But perhaps I was being naïve. Adam

Cummings wasn't being charged with anything, was he? Not as yet, despite the rumblings about Laura Daniels counter-accusing him – was that even a proper legal process?

In any event, there he was, clear as day. Not that there was a lot, to be fair, since I wasn't his 'friend', but, like many people, he hadn't 'locked down' his profile, as Kieron put it, so there were a fair few photos and posts visible to all.

And naturally I was so engrossed that I didn't hear Bella. The first I knew was when she touched me on the shoulder.

'That's my stepdad,' she said.

And since it was too late for burning cheeks and denials, I had no option but to nod and say yes.

I was about to pull together some excuse, but I apparently didn't need one. 'He's called Jacko,' she said, pointing to a face on one of the photos. 'And he's called Griff. He's a bit smelly. He used to come round the house a lot.'

'They're your dad – stepdad's friends, then,' I said, scrolling down to further pictures.

Bella nodded. 'Those are. And those women.' She pointed. 'They're from that club I told you about.'

I scrolled further. And she saw it before I did. Or rather her. 'Is that her?' she asked. 'The woman you were telling me about?' She was indeed. 'She's from his club, too. She's called Cheryl.'

Bella yawned then, unsurprisingly. I turned round in my swivel chair. The blonde woman could wait. 'Look at you,' I said. 'You must be shattered.'

'I'm all right,' she said. 'Sort of.'

'Sort of is the best that can be expected. D'you want some breakfast? You must be starving. Tea was a very long time ago now.'

'Sort of,' she said again. 'But is it all right if I have a bath first?'

'Course you can, sweetheart. Shall I come up and run it for you?'

And to my surprise and delight she said yes.

'You know, it's a big thing you did last night,' I told her, after she'd chosen some special treat bubble bath from the bathroom cabinet. 'But it's going to feel even bigger now, you know that, don't you?'

'I've got to tell, haven't I? Tell a policeman. It's okay. I know that.'

I smiled at her. 'Course you do. You've been told often enough, haven't you? But d'you feel strong enough? They might want you to do that today.'

She nodded. 'That's okay. I don't really care what happens to me now. I'm just glad my mum will be allowed to come home. Even if she *is* cross with me for breaking my promise. Which she shouldn't be – like you said – because I'll explain.'

I had my own take on that; if she was anything like me she'd have been having similar thoughts – that, as a twelve-year-old, Bella was in a highly precarious state. There was no getting away from what she'd physically done, no matter how intense the provocation. And how did you prove it? She didn't have a mark on her. The blows to her stepfather's head came from behind. There was no imme-diate element of self-defence about it.

None of which I was about to share with Bella.

'Exactly,' I said instead. 'And they do say the truth sets you free. So fingers crossed that's what's going to happen to Mum.'

'And I'm okay,' she said again. 'If, you know, they send *me* there.'

'Oh, sweetie,' I said, wrapping my arms tightly round her. 'I know I can't make promises if I'm not absolutely sure, but I am ninety-nine point nine nine nine nine nine certain sure that no one is going to send you away *anywhere*.'

Having left Bella to have her bath, and promised a bacon sandwich on her return, I turned my attention back to the laptop screen. Now I was back to being confused, because Bella clearly knew the woman. Who definitely wasn't an aunt, and, by my reasoning, anyway, was almost certainly a fellow member of Alcoholics Anonymous, and perhaps also part of some splinter support group.

But why lie? What was that about? Did she just think it would make her sound more official? And why did she think she had any right to get involved in the case? But I didn't have a lot of time to ponder her motivation, as my mobile phone started buzzing on the table beside me, the screen announcing a call from John Fulshaw.

'Well, well,' he said. 'We didn't see *that* coming, did we? You okay? Did you get any sleep?'

I told him yes, and a bit, and then we went over Bella's disclosures, which had wrong-footed both him and Kathy – to whom he'd already spoken – as much as me.

'And how's Bella doing?' he asked.

'Okay,' I said, 'though I'm not entirely sure I trust her. She has a good line, I've learned now, in putting on a brave face. In reality? Who knows? Right now she's convinced she's got to take her mum's place, and there's no telling how she'll be when the proverbial hits the proverbial and she has to go through it all again to a stranger.'

'Well, you can probably reassure her on one point. It's almost inconceivable that anyone is going to be taking her anywhere. Chances are, till this is processed, she will stay right where she is.'

'The mysterious blonde sister notwithstanding?' I asked. I couldn't help it. Her pointy face was staring right out of the screen at me. And that second letter had never really been off my mind, either.

'Oh, you can forget her. I just found who she was – when I called the police. And she's no longer a problem. She's been identified and dealt with.'

'What? Well, that's interesting because I just made her virtual acquaintance as it happens.'

'Well I hope you didn't send her a friend request.'

'Of course not. I was just stalking her. The kids would be so proud of me.'

'Well, you need stalk no more. She's just a sometime girlfriend.'

'So she confessed?' I asked.

'She didn't have much choice, I don't think. Not so much a case of exceptional police work as loose lips. She said something to someone who knew someone else who had – has – a lot more time for Laura Daniels than Adam

Cummings. Anyway, I believe she was paid a visit from the boys in blue and I believe she admitted it. And was promptly charged with harassment, you'll be glad to hear.'

I laughed. 'Sounds like something off *EastEnders*.' I also smiled inside. Perhaps the second letter could be quietly forgotten, too. Though it would always have a home in my conscience.

'Anyway, no doubt you'll be hearing about that down the line,' John said. 'And I suspect they'll let her off with a caution. But in the meantime, I'm just waiting for a further call from the family liaison officer, or FLO, to let me know when and where we can all meet.'

When John said 'meet' I knew what he meant. In a case like this, where a child had to be formally interviewed by the police, it was usually arranged to take place at a confidential venue, where she would be interviewed by a police liaison officer (a family liaison officer, often), and her social worker would also be present.

The meeting would also be videoed from another room, in case the child's testimony were needed in court. Not that it was just a case of her being bundled in there, all unsuspecting. Bella would have everything explained to her and would also have to agree to it. There was little doubt she'd be nervous, even scared.

'But you can be there for her before she goes in as well as when she comes out,' John reminded me. 'But you know you're not allowed to sit in on the actual recorded interview, don't you?'

I told him I did, though of course I wished I could. But at least Sophie – who'd be the designated appropriate adult – would be there, and I knew, because this was the sort of thing we had a nodding acquaintance with, that everything would be set up to be warm and unintimidating; would look like an ordinary living room, in fact – anything to put the child at their ease – just with a viewing window for the police officer doing the recording.

'And when Bella confesses to her part – what she did – what then? I know you're confident she won't be taken from us, but will she be charged with anything, given the circumstances and her age?'

John cleared his throat. 'Yes, I think she will be charged,' he said. 'I don't think they have a choice, Casey. It's not up to the police to consider any mitigating circumstances. They'll have to charge her, as she injured somebody, didn't she? And pretty seriously, too. But whether it goes to a youth court or not is an entirely different matter. And in the end, the charges *may* be dropped – all the evidence seems to point to that. But it's not something I can guarantee right now. Not today. And you'll have to explain all that to her – unless you'd rather Sophie did it?'

'No, absolutely. I'll do it. I think it needs to come from me. And I think she'll be okay. Honest, John, she's been poring over enough law books. This won't be any kind of shock.'

So said I. Like I really had any idea.

But, actually, Bella *was* fine. It was as if such an enormous weight had been lifted from her that nothing could get to her. And when I was able to tell her that the 'meeting' was to be that same afternoon at four, I might as well have said she was off to one of Laura's dance

classes, for all the concern she showed. She didn't even
bat an eyelid when I explained about her having to be
charged with a crime. She said she knew all about that
from watching *CSI* with Tyler and that she knew it was all
just 'procedure'.

'Can I take Dobby?' was her only request, and easily
granted. 'I know I'm twelve,' she said solemnly, 'but, well,
you know.'

To my astonishment, the place where the 'meeting' was
being held was barely a mile from our house. Set in the
corner of a council estate I'd visited often over the years,
it was an anonymous-looking semi, at the end of a street,
that you'd never guess was anything other than a normal
family home.

'This is it?' Bella said, peering out of Sophie's
posh tinted windows. 'I thought it would be in a police
station.'

She sounded almost disappointed. To my mind it had
cachet – like something out of a spy thriller. Like a 'safe
house', where people went when in witness protection, to
evade the clutches of gangsters and crooks. I imagined a
sniper on the roof, wielding some extremely high-tech
gun, following the progress of 'perps' in the immediate
area. Though the only current 'perp' was a small tortoise-
shell cat, it didn't matter. The cat could be a plant, and the
whole street staked out. Ooh, I thought, in other circumstances Tyler would love this.

We parked across the road, and I could see Sophie
wrestling with her anxiety. It didn't seem quite the place to
leave such a high-end car. 'Still, if it's safe anywhere on this

estate, it'll be here, don't you think? I expect they keep an eye out 24/7. And I imagine there will be someone who can deal with all comers inside that door, don't you, Bella?'

'Like a soldier?' Bella answered.

'Well, something like that,' Sophie agreed as we climbed out. 'It's got to be secure here, after all.'

'Because of criminals?' Bella asked.

'Well, exactly,' Sophie said. 'This is a top-secret government facility, after all.'

Oh course, Sophie was probably speaking partly in jest, just to keep the tone as light as she could. And of course, I was somewhat going overboard with my imagination – there would be no rooftop gymnastics from Matt Damon here.

But when the door was opened, by a stout lady, wearing a yellow pinny, I think we all did something of a double take.

'My name's Betty,' she said. 'Come in. I've just boiled the kettle. So. Now. Who's up for a brew?'

It was only because she turned around to lead us inside that we managed to keep our giggles out of sight.

Bella was incredibly brave. Though she was pale going into the 'meeting' and clearly anxious about all the strange faces, it ended up being her rather than me doing the reassuring.

'Don't look so worried, Casey,' she said, squeezing my hand. 'I'll be fine.'

Though it was a very different story when she was returned to me. I'd spent an anxious sixty or more minutes, trying to keep myself occupied, and was only partly distracted by conducting a text cookery lesson with Tyler, who was manfully preparing his own tea.

When Bella came out she was in floods again and flung herself at me. But they weren't tears of distress – for once (and it didn't escape me that this was a first since she'd been with us) they were tears of relief.

'I'm okay, I'm okay,' she said, pulling Sophie into our little circle of joy as well. 'I told them all the truth, and they've explained that I had to be arrested, just like you said, but they said it was all right, that I wouldn't be going to prison! Oh, I'm just so happy! I'm not going to jail!'

'See?' I said, as if I'd always known that would happen. But I stopped short of saying 'so everything will be okay now' because that bit I really didn't know.

But the FLO, who was a young woman with a brisk but friendly air, had followed Bella and Sophie out, and now she smiled at me.

'So, I've explained to Bella what will happen now, Mrs Watson, which is essentially that Bella's mum and stepdad are now officially witnesses, and that as soon as the paperwork is written up and dealt with, we will be arranging for her mother's release.'

She leaned down a little to be sure she had Bella's full attention. 'And we've also got a new word in our vocabulary, haven't we, Bella?'

'Corroborate,' Bella supplied, then turned to me. 'Which means they have to get the whole truth from all parties, Casey.'

Exactly,' said the FLO. 'And that has to happen first, of course. Though we're obviously clear it's just a formality.'

'So that's it?' I said. 'I can just take Bella home now?'

'Pretty much,' said the FLO. 'That's it for now, I think. Just make sure you sign out with security before you go.'

AKA Betty. She didn't get why we were grinning either.

Chapter 23

Bella was like a completely different child after giving her recorded statement. A weight had been removed from her shoulders, and it showed. She virtually skipped along beside us back to the car.

Since Tyler had managed to feed himself – well, apparently – without mishap in our absence, I decided I'd take her for tea in our local burger joint as a treat.

'So is that it now, Casey?' she asked as we slurped our milkshakes. 'Will Mum be let out straight away now they know the truth?'

As far as I was concerned, that was what should happen, well, if there was any justice in the world, anyway. They had both suffered enough, after all. She should have been released immediately and their lives allowed to return to normal. Well, as normal as was possible after such a major trauma. But, as we'd already discussed, the wheels of justice didn't move as fast as that, not least because her version of events still needed to be corroborated, as she'd been told.

'I don't think it will be that fast,' I said. 'Remember what the police lady told you? Even though we all know you're telling the truth, another person has to hear your side of the story, and make sure that everything fits together properly. But don't you worry, sweetie. I'm sure it won't be too long.'

'Oh, Casey,' she said, sighing. 'I can't wait. And even if I do get into trouble, it's all okay now, isn't it? Because like Tyler said, the truth sets you free, doesn't it? And I feel free. You know, in here.' She touched her chest. 'So I think he's right.'

I couldn't help but smile. It was me who had told her that, wasn't it? Though perhaps he had as well. It was one of those phrases they loved to use on *CSI*. Perhaps we'd both filed it away for future use. Either way, we had a lot to thank that programme for, I decided. Had she not watched it, would she have had her moment of clarity? Perhaps Grissom had been the one to find the key, not me at all.

Later that night Bella said pretty much the same thing to Tyler, and it struck me how easy the two of them were around each other. How she'd look forward to his return from school, so she could tell him all about her day. And that pleased me hugely, reminding me of what Lauren had pointed out all those weeks ago – that maybe Tyler would always have a special place in her memories.

Tyler himself probably didn't concern himself with such cod psychology. He was way more interested in the business of her having been taken to a 'safe house'. 'Aww, I'm that jealous,' he said, and I watched her puff up with pride. 'You must have felt like you were in a TV cop show yourself.'

Bella considered. 'I suppose I did. Though it was still *mega*-scary. But you were right. I told the truth and it *did* set me free.'

Tyler was olive skinned, Italian-looking, almost, in his colouring. But I was sure I saw a blush darken his cheeks, even so. 'I was only quoting Grissom,' he pointed out. Then he looked at me. 'I wasn't trying to get her to spill, I swear, Mum.'

I couldn't help but laugh. 'Love, it doesn't matter. And besides, that's good advice, so no harm done. All good.'

'Well in that case,' the cheeky sod answered, 'I formally take all credit for solving the case.' I was too busy stifling a laugh to thank him. But he trotted out a 'you're very welcome' even so.

Perhaps one day we'd sit down and I'd have the pleasure of reminding him. Because, actually, he'd probably done more for Bella than he'd ever know.

The next week, predictably, was manic. Nobody knew for sure yet exactly what was going on. Only bits and bats of news filtered through, from John and Sophie, telling us little more than that everything was going to plan.

Not that Laura Daniels was terribly cooperative at first. 'She wouldn't have it,' John told me on the phone a few days later. 'Was still insistent that Bella's version of events was all nonsense, apparently. Stuck to her story. That it was her, and that she'd hit him in self-defence. It took a lot of talking and explaining to get through to her, I'm told. Which is fair enough,' he said. 'Would any parent act differently in her shoes? If there were a shred of doubt that she wouldn't be punished in some way? Let's not forget, this is a family who'd already had several dealings with social services. I'm sure the spectre of Bella being taken from her permanently was ever present. Not to mention having probably picked up all sorts of nonsense about youth detention. You know what it's like, Casey – some people believe anything they read in the tabloids or see on TV.'

I refrained from pointing out that a diet of crime-on-TV 'nonsense' was a Watson family staple. 'I respect her for that,' I said instead.

'Anyway, they got there in the end. Once she understood that Bella wasn't going to be scarred for life by a criminal record, she confessed to everything, and admitted that she'd concocted the story Bella was telling. Well, in this case, *not* telling, of course. The classic silent witness, eh?'

'Well, it certainly says a lot about them, anyway – that Bella didn't waver for so long. I think they'll be all right now. Once this is done with. Don't you?'

John agreed that he did. 'Oh, and she's being moved out of prison in the next couple of days, too. They're going to put her in a halfway house close to home. So I guess we can at least say we are halfway there.'

Bella, when I told her, didn't look quite so jolly. 'What's that?' she asked when I updated her on progress. 'Why can't she just come *home*? That sounds like it's just another prison.'

'It's not, love,' I said. 'It's really not, honestly. She can come and go as she pleases, just like anyone else would. It's just a place where she can be supported while she gets everything straight. There's only one stipulation: that she has to be back at home at a certain time every night. And that's just so they know she's safe – that they always know where she is. It's about looking after her. After all, she's been through a lot, hasn't she?'

Bella nodded. 'Well, that's definitely true.' She was silent a moment then. 'Oh, I wish she could have come and seen Harry Potter with us. It doesn't seem right, all the nice things I've done with you and everyone, and her being locked up and having to eat all that horrible food.'

'Did she tell you that when you visited?' I asked. 'That it was horrible?'

'Beyond horrible,' Bella confirmed. 'She said it was like something out of Dickens.'

'Well, no more,' I reassured her. 'And you know, you'll be able to share all the photos – I'll make sure I print some out for you. And you'll be able to tell her all about our adventures, won't you? Trust me, sweetheart, all that will have mattered to her will have been *your* well-being, not hers. I tell you what, I'll bet she's kept every one of your letters.'

'I've liked writing letters,' Bella said. 'No one does that very much now, do they?'

'Well, why don't you write her one right now?' I suggested. 'Must be time for a sunflower update, don't you think? Oh, and even better news. Sophie's told me you can start visiting her twice a week now –'

'Twice a *week*?'

'Yes, isn't that good?'

But I'd misread her response. 'But that makes it sound like it's going to be ages and ages yet!'

I could see her chin wobbling as she spoke. She was close to crying.

'Sweetie, it's *good* news! It means things are finally moving in the right direction. And yes, it might be a few weeks now, but you have to be patient.'

'But it's not *fair*! It's like she's still being punished, when she didn't even do anything wrong!'

I really could see her point, too. They were both still being punished, where the reality was that the whole tragic episode was not of either of their making, and I had said as much to Sophie myself.

'Well, perhaps she is,' she'd said, her tone philosophical. 'For not walking away from Adam Cummings a long time before. Not that I'm judging her,' she'd added quickly. 'Unless you've been there, how can you possibly know what you'd do? But you see those kinds of toxic cycles again and again, don't you? And it all fits. You know, with the grandfather.'

'What exactly do you know about the grandfather?'

'Not a lot. Just a couple of things Bella's mum has apparently said. I think it was put to her that she might like to build those bridges, and apparently her response was "Why d'you think I got pregnant and got out of there in the first place?" Oh, isn't it the craziest thing that history so often repeats itself? Still, hurrah for the chain breaking. Assuming it stays that way. At least Bella's out of that destructive cycle.'

John, too, was in philosophical mood about everything. In response to my plaintive comment that they were being punished despite being innocent, he was quick to point out that Bella *had* committed a crime.

'Yes, we all know why she did what she did. She reacted impulsively when she thought her mother's life was in serious danger, and did the only thing she could to try and stop it. And there's also the crime of perverting the course of justice, don't forget. If we want the law to be beyond reproach all these things have to be taken seriously, Casey. Now everything has changed from what the law was previously told was the truth, they need to know the physical evidence they have already gathered will fit the new story they have instead. Which is why things take time.' He cleared his throat. 'Sorry. Lecture over.'

Though perhaps it was a lecture that bore repeating, so I did. After all, Bella herself had been keen to make sense of it, and why not add to her education by spelling it out now? Quite apart from anything else, it was education she needed, it having been agreed that it was pointless to start her at our local comp when, all being well, she'd soon be heading home – a place a good way away from us – to take up the reins of her old school life again.

In the meantime, the precious visits to see her mum were our new priority, though my hunch was that it would be better for them to meet on neutral ground. I'd seen a few halfway houses and, though all I'd told Bella was true, they housed all sorts, from vulnerable adults to ex-junkies to all manner of colourful former prisoners, so they could sometimes be less than, well … well-appointed.

* * *

Thankfully, Sophie was all for it. And when we put it to Bella, the following day, she even suggested a place to go. 'From before,' she said. Though before what she didn't say. And we didn't ask. Before *everything*, I guessed. 'It's got a garden, and swings and a climbing frame and everything,' she enthused. 'I think I'm probably too old now for all that,' she mused, 'but, I know! We could take Marley Mae with us, couldn't we?'

No, we couldn't, and wouldn't, because it wouldn't be appropriate. 'And, sweetie,' I pointed out, 'I won't be able to go with you. Sophie will take you. This is all about you spending time with Mum, after all.'

'But I want her to *meet* you,' she insisted.

'Casey, you can come,' Sophie said. 'In fact, John thinks you should. Well, if you want to, that is.'

The unspoken assumption being that, actually, I might like the break. A couple of hours of down time – well, cleaning time, in my case, of course.

But there was no question of me not going once Sophie had said that, and, actually, I did want to meet Laura Daniels. It was one of the little foibles of fostering that you so often found yourself never meeting the parents of the children you cared for. Of ending up with only half the picture. And seeing this mum, in particular, would be a good thing to do. Saying goodbye to vulnerable kids was an emotionally hard business. To know where this one was going could only help smooth the process of letting go. Of *me* letting go.

'Anyway, she's very keen to meet *you*,' Sophie added. 'Not least because she wants the chance to thank you in person. And it'll be a good thing for you too, because you'll know everything's going to be okay when Bella goes.'

They smiled at each other as Sophie said this and I sensed a shared sentiment. What *was* with all this mind-reading people were doing?

I smiled too, sensing the hand of John Fulshaw in the equation. Foster carers didn't routinely get involved in such meetings. That was the job of a child's social worker, always. But John knew me well, and I knew how thoughtful he was. He knew how hard I found the wrench when a child just upped and left. The long goodbye. That was definitely what I was better at.

Chapter 24

'Don't come out yet!' Bella yelled from the back garden. 'And absolutely no peeking!'

Marley Mae giggled, her fists curled into balls and tight against her eyes. 'Nanny, can I look now?' she asked.

It was Saturday morning, and I had a special dispensation to observe, as I'd been busy helping Bella get organised. Later today we would both be off to see her mother, along with Sophie, but right now Mike, Riley, Marley Mae and I were squashed into the conservatory awaiting the big reveal.

Only absent was Tyler, who'd elected to avoid the girly stuff by becoming boy-minder for the morning, taking Levi and Jackson up to the local pitch to watch a 'friendly' football match. Though I never understood why they persisted in calling them that as on the rare occasions I'd been dragged along to them they were anything but. And that included the spectators.

And three out of the four of us were being good and waiting patiently, but as what Marley Mae did know was that the surprise was mostly to be for her it was hardly surprising that she had such ants in her pants.

'Any second now, darling,' I told her, 'and then you can peek.'

'No fair,' she said, her lips pouting, even though she obediently kept her eyes shut. 'I wanna go out *now*.'

'Hey, madam,' Riley scolded, allowing one eye to open slightly, 'less of the attitude or you won't get your surprise at *all*. And I hope this is all worth it, Mother,' she muttered to me. 'Or we'll have a little tantrum on our hands.'

'Don't *worry*,' I reassured her. 'Our little princess is going to love it. It's –'

'Right!' Bella once again bellowed from the garden. 'You can come out now!'

Marley Mae had wriggled out of my grasp even before she'd finished speaking.

Bella was standing proudly by her creation, which was a newly fenced-off corner of my garden, courtesy of the local DIY store. Attached to it was a wooden plaque, which Marley Mae was immediately drawn to. 'Ta dah!' she shouted as we trooped outside.

'Mummy, look!' she cried, squatting down in front of it and clapping her hands together. 'It's got me on! And, look! A princess crown!'

The plaque, which was indeed crown shaped, had been made by one of Mike's work mates for us, and said 'Marley Mae's Sunshine Garden', and beneath it – another squeal of delight from my now hyperventilating granddaughter – were a tiny gardening fork and trowel with pink and yellow handles, and a little yellow bucket and matching watering can.

'It does have your name on it,' Bella said as she knelt down beside Marley Mae. 'And see those teeny tiny green shoots near the back?' She pointed. 'Well, they are your very first sunflowers, already growing. And next week I'm going to help you plant some more, and then some more – that way you'll have a sunshine garden almost to the winter. If you take good care of them, that is. That's what the tools are for. So you can dig up any weeds, and thin them, and water them …'

'All by myself in charge?' Marley Mae said. I could hear Mike chuckle.

'Yes, all by yourself in charge,' Bella said. 'Well, you're almost exactly four now, after all.' She glanced across at me. 'Though if you ask her nicely, I'm sure your nanny will help you. And I'll still be here for a bit. And I'm a sunflower expert. So if you need any advice you can ask me.'

Marley Mae flung her arms around Bella's neck. 'Oh, thank you thank you thank you!' she said. 'My own princess garden! Oh, thank you thank you.' She plastered grateful kisses all over Bella's face. 'And, Nanny, you are allowed to be my special helper. And granddad as well. You can be the very important digger person.'

I could hardly trust myself to speak.

I knew Mike had noticed. 'Happy to take the job, ma'am,' he said. 'Hey, and guess what else, Marley? Me and nanny have bought some special plant pots for Bella to take with her when she goes back home to her mummy, and we've popped some sunflower seeds in those as well.' He smiled at Bella. 'So when she's all settled in she can plant them in *her* garden and you and she can phone each other and tell each other how big they are getting.'

Marley Mae, now sitting on Bella's hip, clapped her hands together again. 'Yes!" she whooped.

'In fact we were thinking you could have a competition,' I told Bella, now I'd managed to compose myself a little. 'See who manages to grow the biggest sunflower. How about that?'

'Oh, that would be ace,' Bella said, furiously tickling Marley now, and I could see she too was fighting not to cry. She put her down then. 'But right now I have to go inside and start getting ready. Why don't you give them a water? I left that job specially for you today, and I bet they're pretty thirsty.'

Then she hurried off indoors, without a backwards glance.

'Oh, bless her,' Riley said, twisting to watch her going inside. 'She's really upset.'

'It's been an emotional morning, and it's going to be an emotional afternoon,' I said, as Mike and Marley went to fill up her dinky watering can.

'You can say that again,' Riley said. 'God, can you imagine what it must have been like having to see her in that place? Thank God that ordeal is over at least.'

'And a big change coming up,' I said. 'A happy change in this case. But it's still a big transition to make. I hate it too. It's the worst thing in the world, isn't it?' I knew Riley understood because though she was still mostly doing respite work, she had lived our fostering lives with us so closely. And wasn't that the rub of it? That the better things went, and the closer you became to a child, the more you had to suffer for your fostering 'success'?

I followed her inside. She'd dried her tears by the time I'd found her in the downstairs cloakroom, and was busy blowing her nose. 'So much crying!' she observed, giving me a wan smile once she'd finished.

'You and me both, sweetie,' I told her. 'Not to mention Mike.'

'*Mike* was crying?' This made her smile widen.

'Only in secret,' I told her. 'So don't tell.'

Sophie arrived on the dot of two, just after we'd finished a quick sandwich lunch, and Tyler, now home, had been given his very important warnings about the sanctity of the hallowed princess space and how no ball of any kind must ever breach its boundaries. (Yeah, right, I thought. Like that was going to be in any way manageable. Happily, however, I also knew sunflowers – and a tougher, more resilient-stemmed annual you'd never see.)

Mike was first out of the front door to greet her – or, more accurately her lovely car, which, in that way that men do, he, once given permission, observed from all angles, standing, arms folded across his chest, pointing out its many features to Tyler, and peering closely at the perfect finish on the paintwork.

While Bella ran in to grab the photographs the printer was finishing printing out for her, Sophie and I stood and watched, amused, on the doorstep.

'He's in love,' I said.

She grinned. 'I'm still a little bit in love with her too,' she confessed. 'Which is a new one on me. I've never really been much of a car person at all. An A to B – or rather "A to grim council flat on the edge of the red light district" person, given the job. You know how it is.'

'Really?' I said, still bemused at why and how this still so young social worker (not the best-paid job in the world) had ownership of such a swanky expensive car. It was perplexing. A sugar daddy? I dismissed the thought immediately. Sophie was the very antithesis of a sugar-daddy type. And thank the lord for that.

So I thought I'd ask her. Why not, after all?

'If it's not too presumptuous a question,' I went on, 'how come you are driving around in that beauty, then?'

She turned and smiled at me. 'I think it's what's called an impulse purchase.'

'Some impulse purchase!'

She laughed. 'No, it really was! When Mum died, it turned out that she had taken out this life-insurance policy that no one knew about – certainly not Dad; though she was a pretty high-up civil servant and she'd always been sensible like that – and I found myself sitting on a big wodge of unexpected cash, so ...' She spread her arms. 'Mad, eh? I know I should have put it in some sensible high-interest bank account, or used it as a deposit on a flat or something – and there's still a little bit left for that. Well, a teeny bit. But, you know – I needed to change my old banger, and I kept looking at sensible replacements, and then one day I just woke up – I'd been dreaming about Mum, I think – and I thought sod it. I'm going to have something completely indulgent. Because I kept thinking of what Mum said while she was dying. Do it now. You never know what's going to happen. Do it *now*. So I did. Because you don't ever know, do you? What's coming up round the corner ... Oh, Christ, sorry ...' She waved a hand in front of her face. 'Sorry ... I've started myself off now ...'

'Blinking heck,' I said. 'And now you've started me off, and all.'

Thankfully, Bella was way too excited on the journey to set off any further bouts of crying, and, happily, the journey this time was much shorter.

We arrived at a large sprawling pub on the far edge of town just half an hour later.

'Ooh, look, kids eat free,' Sophie observed. 'Wonder if I'll be able to hoodwink them.'

We all clambered out. Being a Saturday, and a sunny spring one, it was busy, but also enormous, a giant-sized rabbit warren of eating areas, play areas, picnic tables and an enormous soft play zone, to boot, and I made a mental note that this would be a great place to take the family. But today was about reuniting another family, that of the smiling but growing nervous now twelve-year-old whose hand was in mine.

Though not for long. I knew we'd found the right person before I even saw her because that same little hand slipped suddenly from mine and Bella was off towards the woman who was waving manically at her. 'Mummy!' she cried as she launched herself at her. 'Mummy, Mummy, Mummy!', plastering the same kisses on her mother's face as Marley Mae had on hers. It hit me forcibly then just how much of a child our stoic little visitor really was. And had to try not to cry all over again.

'You'd match them in a line-up, wouldn't you?' Sophie whispered, as we watched Bella's progress to the main pub dining area and, finally, into the arms of her mother. She was right. Even if I hadn't seen a photograph, I'd have identified her immediately. She had the same hair and eyes, and the same sort of build, though her ordeal certainly showed in her gauntness.

We both hung back, so they could have some time alone.

'And, you know, you can just tell what a good mum she is, can't you?' Sophie said quietly. 'I could see it when I saw them in the prison together, but now she doesn't have to watch what she's saying, it's even more obvious. You know what I mean? That connection.'

I nodded. 'I don't think I ever doubted it,' I said. 'Bella clearly loves her mother. And her mother was simply doing what she thought was right. Protecting her daughter, and at potentially huge cost to herself. Can you imagine if he *had* died? God, how different things could have been. I can't blame her for anything, truth be known. Just the enormity of it all clouded everybody's judgement.'

'Speaking of judgements, I have some news on that front actually,' Sophie said. 'I thought I'd wait till we all got settled and then I can update you all together. Come on, let's get a table so we can sit down and discuss it.'

It was the best news Bella could be given. After all the introductions, understandably fulsome and emotional, and the food order (spookily we all ordered the same – chilli and chips), we were settled at our table with our drinks, and Sophie ran through the next steps.

And on what I'd prepared Bella would probably be quite a long journey. And which, happily, she was coming to accept as a reality that wouldn't be the end of the world. Not least because almost the first thing Laura Daniels said to me was, 'I could cry knowing she's with you while all this is ongoing. I cannot begin to tell you how grateful I am to you all.' And then *she* started crying, which set us all off. I knew then that she'd been briefing Bella on the journey herself.

'I have been in touch with the council on your behalf,' Sophie told Laura now. 'And for once – praise the deities – luck is on your side. As you probably already knew, Adam – your ex … [A pause. Tricky to know how to refer to him.] … Bella's stepfather went to stay with a friend [the lovely Cheryl? I'd take a punt on it.] after leaving hospital, and has now moved completely out of the area.' Laura Daniels nodded. 'But what you might not yet know,' she went on, 'is that, fortunately for you, he forgot to inform the council that he was going.'

I watched Laura squeeze Bella's hand as this news began sinking in. 'So the joint tenancy –'

'Is still in place,' Sophie confirmed.

She went on to explain, probably as much for my benefit as anything, that in other circumstances by being in prison Laura would have lost her entitlement to the house – it would have automatically transferred to the joint tenant, in this case Adam Cummings. But because Adam never removed his own name from the tenancy, and Laura had now been released, she could now legally take it back as a sole tenant. 'Well, so long as you get an arrangement in place to repay the arrears that have obviously mounted up. But don't worry,' she went on. 'It only has to be a very small amount each month. And if you struggle, you can apply for extra housing benefit, given your circumstances. So that's good, isn't it?'

Laura hooked her fingers beneath Bella's chin. 'What do you think, Bella Boo? Would you be okay about going back to our old house, do you think? Because it's okay if you're not. If it's too difficult, you know, because of everything that happened. Don't want you having nightmares ...'

Bella flapped a dismissive hand. 'I'll be *fine*, Mummy!' she reassured her. 'Course I'm okay about it! I'd hate to move anywhere else. It's our house and always will be. It's *home*. Our home. You and me.' (She didn't say what I'm sure we were all thinking – without *him* there.) 'Anyway, I'd hate to move anywhere away from Ruby and all my other friends. We have to go back there. So this is *mega*.'

'Mega?' Laura Daniels asked. 'What's mega when it's at home?'

A little something from Tyler, to take away with her, I thought happily.

And along with the chilli came yet more good news. Because Adam had more or less admitted that he never knew for sure who had hit him – too drunk to remember, as borne out by his blood alcohol levels – the evidence was now being re-examined, and much discounted (including the name-calling by nosey neighbours? I hoped so), and it would only be a matter of days now before Laura was allowed to leave the halfway house and return home.

So all that preparation for the long haul, and it had suddenly become short haul. Oh, my, I thought. To-do list time again.

'And what about Bella? Will she have anything on her record?' Laura asked Sophie. 'Because if she gets into trouble, or ends up with a criminal record, then all of this will have been for nothing.'

Again Sophie smiled. 'Her stepfather has already said that if it was Bella, then he wouldn't press charges, and I don't think the courts will want to either, to be honest, because if it's all proven in your favour, Laura, then Bella was simply trying to save you from harm and can't really be accountable for her actions that night. Anyway, hopefully, in the next few days we'll all know for sure, and then that really will be the end of it.'

'Amen to that,' I said, digging in.

The hour and a half agreed upon was soon over. Funny, I thought, as we licked the last of our ice-cream bowls clean, to think that to any casual observer we must look like any random group of females, out for a girly lunch. Mum and daughter, and, in Sophie and me, perhaps mum and daughter also – she was certainly dark haired and young enough to have been mine. Though a good deal taller, which, admittedly, wasn't difficult.

Yet around that table sat a shared experience most would – thankfully – never find themselves involved in. It certainly made you wonder. What stories were being played out or recalled on other tables? Everyone had one, after all.

Before we left, and after a very emotional farewell between Bella and her mother, Laura thanked me profusely again, while Sophie and Bella went to the loo for the journey. Laura herself was being picked up by her mother. I wanted so much to ask her about all that but didn't. We were now *truly* in the realm of 'none of my business'.

She thanked me, fulsomely and emotionally, for taking care of her baby, for believing in her, for encouraging her to do the right thing. 'I was too blinded by fear to do that,' she said. 'And I truly thought I was doing what was best for her. Wrong,' she said. 'So wrong. She'd have been haunted by it always. It would have destroyed her.' She shook her head. 'But you know what? In that moment I'd have done the same again. What mother wouldn't?'

'Exactly,' I agreed.

Laura Daniels sighed. She had expressive eyes, and I could see the guilt in them. Something I supposed, and hoped, would lessen once they got their lives back on track. 'She never asked for any of this, did she?' she said. 'That's why. She never asked to be involved in such an abusive relationship, did she? That was all *my* doing. It's scary, really, how history repeats itself, isn't it? I'm sure you must have seen it yourself, often, being a foster mum. And you know the worst of it? That my biggest fear in life was making a life for my child that was like the one I had. With a father like I had ...' She looked past me. 'Yet here we are. I bloody managed to find one anyway. But no more.' She smiled then, unexpectedly. 'Speak of the devil.' She raised an arm and waved. 'My mother. Bless her,' she said. 'But no more.'

Chapter 25

I believed in Laura Daniels. Just as she'd thanked me for believing in her daughter (a concept that still perplexed me – how else should an adult relate to a child? But then I hadn't grown up with Laura Daniels's father, had I?), I believed she would do exactly what she'd promised: break the cycle so her own daughter had a different, better life.

Yes, it might be that, down the line, she met another challenging man, but there can be few wake-up calls as loud as a spell in prison, contemplating a future behind bars and a daughter scarred for life. No, on balance, I'd lay odds that Laura Daniels would be fine.

In the short term, the leaving day, I knew I would not be fine. Yes, I'd be fine in the long term – given the happiness of this particular leave-taking, I knew I'd probably perk up by the end of the day. I had sunflowers to keep an eye on, after all – but right now, on this cloudy Wednesday, with us all crowded by the front gate, I went with the flow, because there was nothing else for it. I was wet inside and very soon wet on the outside, as the tears tracked unhindered down my cheeks. ('So much crying!' as Bella had so recently observed.)

Mike wasn't crying, but once again he was drooling, as Sophie's sleek BMW sat and dozed by the kerb, like a supermodel enjoying a quick fag break.

Bella was all togged out in the plum-coloured dress she loved so much, and about which I'd revised my original opinion. It suited her perfectly. I wondered what would become of her, this clever little thing – something great, something learned, I had no doubt of it. In the meantime, she was twelve, though, and clutching her Dobby, telling Mike to tell Ty (again) how much she'd loved all the mega times they'd had and how they'd become friends on Facebook.

Tyler himself wasn't there. It was a school day, for starters, but though I told him he'd be allowed to take the morning off, he'd declined, saying he didn't want to do all the goodbye stuff. Instead, they'd had their farewell moment over breakfast before he'd left for school. And he had set off with tears in his own eyes. I couldn't wait to have him home again at teatime. I never could.

'And everyone else,' Bella said now, including us all in her glance. 'And Kieron and Lauren – oh, I'm so sorry I never made it to Lauren's dance class. And I promise, Casey, I will phone you every week.'

I said I'd love that. Though ideally I hoped that, before too long, it would dwindle to a more manageable once a fortnight, then once a month, because, much as I'd miss her, then I'd know she'd moved on with her life.

She handed Dobby to Marley Mae ('Not to keep,' she warned, 'just so I can give you a proper hug.') and picked her up, swinging her right up above her shoulders. 'And I shall Facetime you, my little princess, so we can compare our sunflowers, okay? Now, quick, give me kisses before I have to go.'

Riley squeezed my hand, and I'm quite sure she nipped me a little to try to stop me full-on blubbing like a baby, as we watched little Marley smother Bella in wet kisses.

Bella put her back down, retrieved Dobby (who I could even now see accompanying her to some great seat of learning, and being propped in front of the pillows on some hall of residence bed) and then turned to hug me again. 'I have to go now,' she said, 'but please say goodbye to everyone else for me. I'm going to really miss you. *All* of you.'

I kissed the top of her head, which smelt of my favourite shampoo. 'Go on, sweetie,' I whispered. 'We'll see you again, I'm sure. Now go get in the car before you start me off again.'

'I'm going to miss that car,' Mike said, as we clustered around it, while Bella climbed in and belted up, and Sophie shut the door.

Sophie winked at me. 'Do it now,' she said. We both laughed.

'What?' Mike said.

'Do it *now*,' Sophie said again.

'What, buy a car like yours?' he said, the penny dropping. 'I flipping *wish*.'

He plunged a hand into his jeans pockets, pulled it out and inspected it. Then motioned that I should open my hand.

I did so and he placed couple of pound coins into it. 'There you go,' he said. Now it was my turn to look confused. 'What's this for?'

'Definitely won't be enough to buy a car, Dad,' Riley said.

'No, but it'll be enough for your mum to buy a couple of lottery tickets with.'

Bella had already opened the car window and now she held one of Dobby's hands out of it.

'Car-eeee-amus get-eeee-armus!' she said dramatically, as she waved it. Then she grinned.

'I know he's only a house elf, but you never know!'

Epilogue

In the end, to everyone's relief, Bella's evidence wasn't even required. There was no day in court for her because there was no day in court.

Adam Cummings, it seemed, was a rare beast. His brush with death had clearly given him a new and welcome perspective, and once informed of Bella's disclosures he formally retracted his earlier statement. He also admitted that while he'd been sure it had been his wife who had hit him initially, if Bella said it had been her then it obviously must have been. After all, as he'd pointed out to his lawyer, she had been the only sober person in the room.

To Bella's great delight, it had also been 'corroborated forensically'. She'd been able to describe the events of that night in great detail, and her evidence, that her mother had actually been pinned *beneath* her stepfather (and also where), was borne out by the pattern of blood marks on the floor. She'd been thrilled when the family liaison officer had conveyed this to her. 'You know what?' I told her in letter I wrote to her. 'I think you should consider a career in the law.' She responded quickly. 'No! I'm going to be a detective!'

Bella's stepfather's greatest move, though, was to move right away and stay away. Yes, he'd dried out, and had no intention of drinking again, ever, but that in itself posed a great risk – of the cycle repeating itself, should Bella's mother give him yet another chance, which was the last thing Bella wanted, or needed, in the world. As it was, mother and daughter moved back home together and, to date, have been settled and well.

No more was ever heard of the sister-impersonating Cheryl, other than, sadly, she'd stopped going to AA. Out of sight, definitely in my case, very much out of mind. I had done a stupid, unprofessional thing and didn't I know it? I'd been very lucky not to have it come back and bite me on the bottom, something that, with hindsight, I reflected on at length. I wasn't sure that I'd never do something like it again, but I hoped not, which, when dealing with high stakes and emotions, was really all you could do.

The sunflowers grew. And grew. And grew. By that August the tallest of the ones growing in 'Marley Mae's sunshine garden' was, at our best guess, some eleven feet tall. We kept a diary, and took pictures, as did Bella, with her own plants. In the end we agreed on a draw.

I got my karaoke machine out on my birthday. ☺

TOPICS FOR READING-GROUP DISCUSSION

1. Social Services are often caught between the devil and the deep blue sea – damned if they do and damned if they don't. In Bella's case, do you think she should have been taken into care sooner? Or do you think pre-emptive action of that kind risks encroaching on families' civil liberties?

2. At what age do you think that children should be deemed criminally responsible for their actions? Should 'extenuating circumstances' be given more credence with regard to children, and if so, why?

3. When you consider the significant resources used to prosecute an offender, such as the costs of remanding and defending, do you believe that in a case like this the mother should have faced other charges?

4. From this case, what do you think might happen with Bella in the future? Under what circumstances might this manifest? What should be done to minimise the impact of her early years' trauma?

5. Alcohol is often a factor in the breakdown of family life. As a society, do you think we should be doing more to tighten the rules around its availability and in deciding licensing laws? Or do you feel this will only criminalise addicts further?

CASEY WATSON

One woman determined to
make a difference.

Read Casey's poignant
memoirs and be inspired.

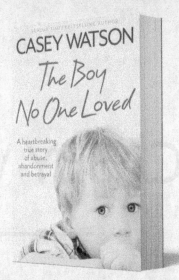

Five-year-old Justin was desperate and helpless

Six years after being taken into care, Justin has had 20 failed placements. Casey and her family are his last hope.

THE BOY NO ONE LOVED

A damaged girl haunted by her past

Sophia pushes Casey to the limits, threatening the safety of the whole family. Can Casey make a difference in time?

CRYING FOR HELP

Abused siblings who do not know what it means to be loved

With new-found security and trust, Casey helps Ashton and Olivia to rebuild their lives.

LITTLE PRISONERS

Branded 'vicious and evil', eight-year-old Spencer asks to be taken into care

Casey and her family are disgusted: kids aren't born evil. Despite the challenges Spencer brings, they are determined to help him find a loving home.

TOO HURT TO STAY

A young girl secretly caring for her mother

Abigail has been dealing with pressures no child should face. Casey has the difficult challenge of helping her to learn to let go.

MUMMY'S LITTLE HELPER

Two boys with an unlikely bond

With Georgie and Jenson, Casey is facing her toughest test yet.

BREAKING THE SILENCE

A teenage mother
and baby in need of
a loving home

At fourteen, Emma is just
a child herself – and one
who's never been properly
mothered.

A LAST KISS FOR MUMMY

Eleven-year-old Tyler
has stabbed his
stepmother and has
nowhere to go

With his birth mother
dead and a father
who doesn't want him,
what can be done to stop
his young life spiralling
out of control?

NOWHERE TO GO

What is the secret behind Imogen's silence?

Discover the shocking and devastating past of a child with severe behavioural problems.

THE GIRL WITHOUT A VOICE

Kiara appears tired and distressed, and the school wants Casey to take her under her wing for a while

On the surface, everything points to a child who is upset that her parents have separated. The horrific truth, however, shocks Casey to the core.

A STOLEN CHILDHOOD

Flip is being raised by her alcoholic mother, and comes to Casey after a fire at their home

Flip has Foetal Alcohol Syndrome (FAS), but it soon turns out that this is just the tip of the iceberg . . .

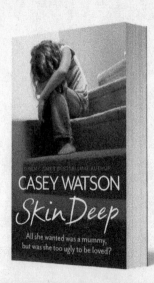

SKIN DEEP

Leo isn't a bad lad, but his frequent absences from school mean he's on the brink of permanent exclusion

Leo is clearly hiding something, and Casey knows that if he is to have any kind of future, it's up to her to find out the truth.

MUMMY'S LITTLE SOLDIER

Adrianna arrives on Casey's doorstep with no possessions, no English and no explanation

It will be a few weeks before Casey starts getting the shocking answers to her questions . . .

RUNAWAY GIRL

AVAILABLE AS E-BOOK ONLY

Cameron is a sweet boy who seems happy in his skin – making him rather different from most of the other children Casey has cared for

But what happens when Cameron disappears? Will Casey's worst fears be realised?

JUST A BOY

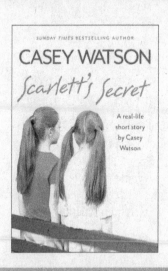

Jade and Scarlett, seventeen-year-old twins, share a terrible secret

Can Casey help them come to terms with the truth and rediscover their sibling connection?

SCARLETT'S SECRET

AVAILABLE AS E-BOOK ONLY

Nathan has a sometime alter ego called Jenny who is the only one who knows the secrets of his disturbed past

But where is Jenny when she is most needed?

Secrets always find a way of revealing themselves, sometimes you just need someone to talk to

No Place for Nathan

A SHORT STORY

CASEY WATSON

SUNDAY TIMES BESTSELLING AUTHOR

NO PLACE FOR NATHAN

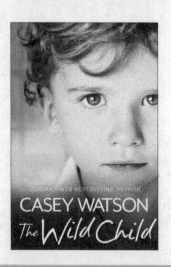

SUNDAY TIMES BESTSELLING AUTHOR

CASEY WATSON

The Wild Child

Angry and hurting, eight-year-old Connor is from a broken home

As streetwise as they come, he's determined to cause trouble. But Casey is convinced there is a frightened child beneath the swagger.

THE WILD CHILD

AVAILABLE AS E-BOOK ONLY

Six-year-old Darby is naturally distressed at being removed from her parents just before Christmas

And when the shocking and sickening reason is revealed, a Happy New Year seems an impossible dream as well . . .

THE LITTLE PRINCESS

Adam is brought to Casey while his mum recovers in hospital – just for a few days

But a chance discovery reveals that Casey has stumbled upon something altogether more sinister . . .

AT RISK

FEEL HEART.
FEEL HOPE.
READ CASEY.

Discover more about Casey Watson.
Visit www.caseywatson.co.uk

Find Casey Watson on &